Today's Revival Stories

Fanning the Flames of Revival

Other books by Pamela Bolton:

Ushering in Revival and Awakening—Fanning the Flames of Revival

God on the Move—Fanning the Flames of Revival

Circuit Riders—Fanning the Flames of Revival

Lady Preachers—Fanning the Flames of Revival

Today's Glory Stories—Fanning the Flames of Revival

Black Lives Made a Difference—Fanning the Flames of Revival (By Pamela Bolton and Dean Braxton)

Today's Revival Stories

Fanning The Flames Of Revival

By Pamela Bolton

Copyright © 2025 by Pamela Bolton
Today's Revival Stories
Fanning the Flames of Revival
by Pamela Bolton
Printed in the United States of America

1st Edition
ISBN: 978-1-7349220-4-2

All rights reserved. The author guarantees all contents are original and do not infringe upon the legal rights of any other person or work. No part of this publication may be reproduced or transmitted in any form or by any means, electronic or mechanical, including photocopying, recording, or any information storage or retrieval system, without the permission in writing from the author.

All scripture quotations are taken from the
King James Version
or the New King James Version of the Bible
Copyright © 1982 by Thomas Nelson, Inc.,
Nashville, Tennessee, United States of America

http://www.pamelabolton.com
http://outoftheboxworshipcenter.com

TODAY'S REVIVAL STORIES

FANNING THE FLAMES OF REVIVAL

Contents

DEDICATION..
FOREWORD...
INTRODUCTION...

1. My Passion for Revival & Awakening 1
2. Preparation, News Articles, and Advertising 27
3. Bishop Lance Johnson's Account...................................53
4. Revival Stories Look What the Lord Has Done!.........57
5. Pastor's Revival Perspectives 67
6. Worship Team Perspectives 83
7. Follow-up News Articles 89
8. Photo Album 105
9. Now What? 115

THANK YOU! 119
IN CLOSING...121

DEDICATION

This book is dedicated to all of you who have faithfully prayed and cried out to God for full-blown revival and awakening… and to all the pastors, leaders, and volunteers who helped make the Awake America Crusade happen. It would not have been possible without your help and support. Today, God is looking for those who have a passion for more of Him above all else, and I believe this includes many of you.

OUT OF THE BOX WORSHIP CENTER CRUSASDE PRAYER TEAM

My sincere appreciation to each of you who met faithfully for many months to intercede and pray for a mighty move of God in Whitehall and the surrounding areas along the NY/VT border. I cannot THANK YOU all enough!

Donna LaPierre
(Worship Leader)
Patricia Medina
Terri Book
Barbara Levesque
Laurie Donaldson
Schuyler Schieffelin

Jennifer Brooks
Bonnie Rajah
Jef Bourn
Paul and Suzanne Bendick
Elizabeth Bates
Barry and Evie Dean

May God grant that you continue to see the answers to your prayers! He is able to do exceedingly and abundantly more that you can ask, think, or even imagine, according to His power that is at work within us… especially through our prayers. (Ephesians 3:20 & James 5:16b-18)

Never underestimate what God can do in and through your life. Nothing is impossible for Him!

Foreword

Pastor Pamela Bolton has done a remarkable job of capturing both the heart and the works of God in Upstate New York and throughout the Northeast. In these pages, she not only shares firsthand accounts of this powerful move of God but also traces the history and events that helped spark it. With her unique gift for conveying spiritual insight with clarity and depth, Pastor Bolton brings to life the moments of God's presence in a way that will stir your hunger for Him and deepen your resolve to contend for revival.

This book is more than a record—it is a guide. It lays out a clear pathway and pattern for revival that will inspire all who long for His glory and for a fresh move of His Spirit. May it ignite faith and passion in every reader to believe for awakening in our nation and beyond.

Bishop Lance Johnson
Relevate Church, Ranger, GA

INTRODUCTION

God is on the Move here in the Northeast, and we get to be a part of what He's doing right here, right now! This is such an exciting time to be alive, and it is so awesome to see God answering our prayers in real time. We are experiencing what many others had prayed for all their lives and never saw on this side of Heaven.

In this book, I hope to share with you some of the testimonies of those whose lives were forever changed at the Awake America Crusade as well as my small part of the story of how we got there.

I am so looking forward to seeing what God has in store for us as we see His plans unfold. There are fires springing up all over our region, and lives are being changed for the glory of God. Unbelievers are coming into the knowledge of the truth. Many are being saved, and many are recommitting their lives to the Lord. God is drawing people to Himself, and Jesus is touching and healing hearts and changing lives. Believers are being refreshed and revived.

What more could we want?
What more could we ask for?

This is what many of us have desired to see happen for decades! This is what we were believing God for. This is it! It's the real deal!

Now is the time to press in in prayer even more so than ever before, trusting God for even greater things today!

KEEP PRAYING & STAY HUNGRY!

PLEASE NOTE: Some minor grammatical and spelling errors were corrected from the original newspaper articles and people's stories, for clarity.

Chapter 1

My Passion For Revival & Awakening

THE AWAKE AMERICA CRUSADE

What did God do at the Awake America Crusade? I want to begin by sharing just one person's powerful testimony of how this Crusade impacted his life. This was written by a pastor whom I've known for close to 17 years. Many more testimonies will follow later in this book.

"I've lived in rural upstate New York for 17 years. I have never seen anything like this. This is not a professional, organized, religious event. This is a family on fire, crying out for the healing love of God to shine on a starving generation.

If you're a church goer, please, don't pass this off. Don't criticize it. How many wonderful souls have built churches and watched them die? I listened to an 80-year-old man (Rev. Harlow Gordon) *with tears in his eyes tell me how much it meant to him to see people in his church again. How many of our grandparents in the faith longed to see churches resurrected?*

"Let go of the criticism, bitterness, jealousy, and open your souls to the awakenings like those during the times of Wesley. Don't try to figure it out, dissect it, criticize it, or control it. Learn,

listen, and trust God. He knows how to lead His children. God, open our hearts that we might see your love and obey the lifelong call to give that love.

"Lance Johnson said it best. 'I thought it was up to me to find God, but what I discovered is that it was God who found me.'

"Jesus, Do what only you can do."
Pastor Jason Proctor
Camden United Methodist Church, NY
Cleveland United Methodist Church, NY

HOW DID THIS HAPPEN?

My passion to see full-blown revival and awakening in our day began about 25 years ago when I watched a documentary entitled, *Transformations*, by George Otis, Jr. The film showed how when the people of God joined together to worship Him in one accord, He transformed their cities and towns - in Colombia, Kenya, Guatemala, and the United States. When I was watching this for the first time, tears were pouring down my face, and I knew that I knew that this was God's heart for us today.

I began to read about many of the old revivals that had taken place around the world… and about the people that God chose to use to bring them about - Charles Finney (New York State), Evan Roberts (Welsh Revival), Peggy and Christine Smith (Hebrides Revival), William Seymour (Azuza Street Revival), and many more. I devoured the *God's Generals* books by Roberts Liardon. I noticed that the men and women that God chose to use were all very different from one another, but the one thing they had in common was their passion for more of God in their lives, along with their desire to see His will accomplished on the planet in their day. Many of them prayed earnestly to see God move in power, and as I read their stories, I realized that we had to do the same thing today if we wanted to witness the same results.

Over the years, I watched that *Transformations* documentary close to 20 times, and almost every time that I watched it, the same thing happened. Tears would steam down my face. I couldn't stop them. It was like the Holy Spirit was touching my heart in a very real and powerful way over and over again, showing me that God wanted this more than we did. This was His heart for prior generations, but it is also His heart for our generation.

I knew that God was not a respecter of persons, and if he wasn't, then if we did what they did, He would move in mighty power again in our day. Even though it might not look the same as in prior moves of His Spirit, it would still be wonderful.

Out of the Box Worship Center was founded in June 2013, under the covering of Living Waters Evangelistic Ministries, which is based out of Cambridge, NY. From its inception, we brought in many guest speakers that helped pave the way for what God wanted to do at this Crusade. Dean Braxton was especially influential due to the message that he brought as well as by helping us make connections with many, many pastors and ministries in the area.

In 2019, God placed it on my heart to hold a prayer event and invite pastors, leaders, and their congregations to the Old Brick Church between Whitehall, NY and Poultney, VT. We prayed on the grounds for weeks beforehand, but during the final week, we prayed inside the church almost every day.

From my research at the local library, I knew that revival had broken out in that very church and on the grounds in the late 1800s. We were expecting God to move in power again, and He did. The moment people stepped inside the church, they could sense the presence of God in a very real and tangible way.

We were so pleased when approximately 100 people showed up to worship in one accord, and there were 17 pastors in attendance from different denominations… Presbyterians, Catholics, Pentecostals, Baptists (Southern and American), and Lutherans all worshipping the Lord together in one accord. This was the beginning of a series of eleven prayer events that Out of the Box Worship Center organized at different locations between June of 2019 and June 2025.

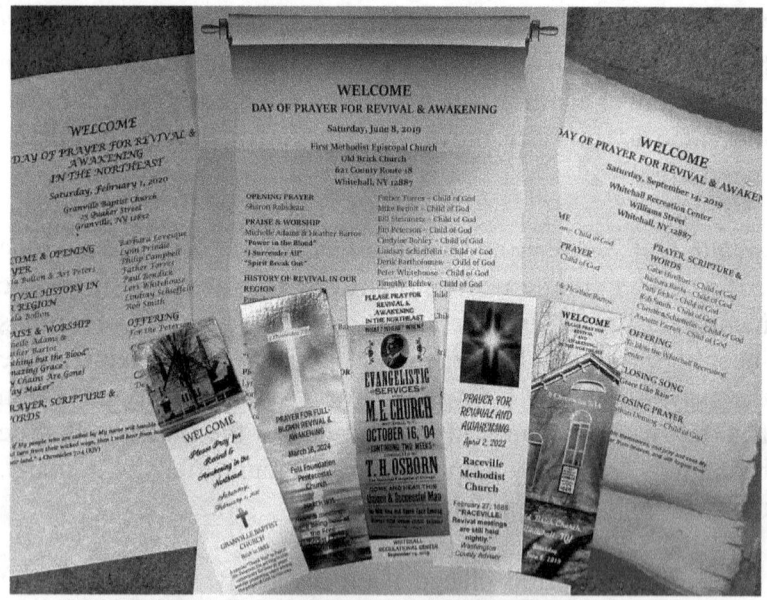

SOME DETAILS ABOUT PRAYER EVENTS HELD BETWEEN JUNE 8, 2019 - JUNE 28, 2025

LEFT: PROPHETIC PHOTO TAKEN THROUGH WINDOW
RIGHT: OLD BRICK CHURCH, WHITEHALL

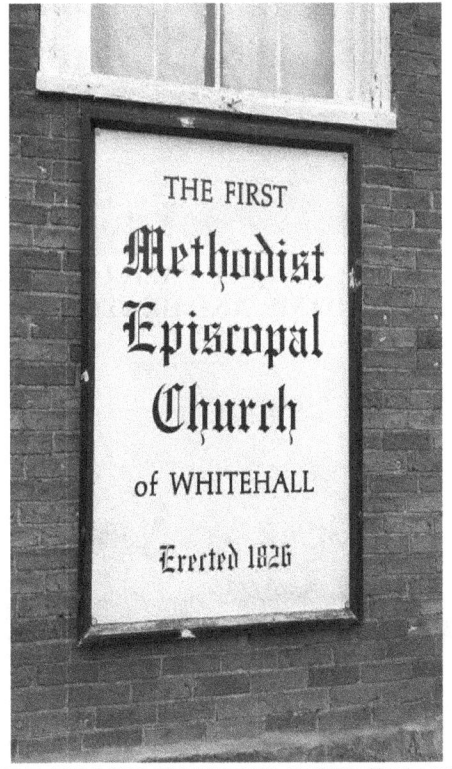

OLD BRICK CHURCH, WHITEHALL

JUNE 8, 2019 - PASTOR PAMELA BOLTON, MICHELLE ADAMS, AND HEATHER BARTOS

JUNE 8, 2019 - OLD BRICK CHURCH MEETING

OLD BRICK CHURCH MEETING

JUNE 8, 2019 – PRAYER MEETING AT THE OLD BRICK CHURCH IN WHITEHALL, NY (excerpts from *Ushering in Revival and Awakening – Fanning the Flames of Revival*)

When I finally stood up, I looked out at the people; and I thought to myself, "How did we get here? This is the answer to so many prayers, some even prayed going back to two-hundred years ago. God is so pleased with this!" It was overwhelming, and I had to hold back tears of joy as I realized that we were not only watching history in the making, but we were a part of it ... history that made a mark for all of eternity. What an overwhelming thought!

For some other pastors, and men and women of God in our area, it was what they've desired for years too. There were many believers, including pastors, from different denominations and churches from our region, all worshiping God together in unity. It was so wonderful to finally see people coming together for Jesus and Him alone. They didn't come with their own agendas but solely to praise, worship, and pray in one accord.

DIGGING UP LOCAL, OLD WELLS OF REVIVAL

OUR STORY
Prayer Service at Old Brick Church, June 8, 2019

In August of 2018, I felt that God was impressing me to go to our local Historical Society in Whitehall, NY, to see what I could find out about prior times of Revival and Awakening in our area. My passion was to find out what God had done in our little community in the past. I knew that He is not a respecter of persons (Acts 10:34), so if He did something for some people in our little town years ago, He'd do it for us, too. I found newspaper clippings about revivals that had taken place in our area. There is one church in particular that I found a lot of information about – The Methodist Episcopal Church (hereafter referred to as Old Brick Church) in East Whitehall, NY.

During the fall of 2018, I felt that God was directing me to ask to hold a special prayer meeting at this small, old country church that is located just a few miles outside of our village. Currently, there is only one service a year held there, and the church doesn't have any electricity or running water.

I asked the Old Brick Church board if we could use the property for a one-day prayer event, and after they asked me several questions, they approved our request. I was told by a lifetime resident of our community that we had found favor, but I didn't realize the extent of what that meant until later.

One day, I stopped by the Old Brick Church to thank one of the board members who was working outside on a restoration project. He told me that he couldn't remember a time when that church had allowed ANY group to use that building other than family members or friends for weddings and funerals.

I just knew that God had planned this service; it was to be a special, divine appointment. Over the next several months, we went out to the property and prayed over it numerous times. We were digging up the old wells of revival in our area and petitioning Heaven for fresh Living Water.

On Saturday, June 8, 2019, we had a wonderful prayer service. We were blessed to have at least 17 pastors and 15 different churches in attendance. Denomination wise, we know that there were people from each of following churches as well as several independent churches: Presbyterian, Catholic, Assemblies of God, Lutheran, American Baptist, Southern Baptist, Congregational, and Independent Assemblies of God. The Episcopal and Methodist pastors wanted to attend, but they weren't able to due to prior commitments. We all worshiped and prayed together in unity, and the presence of God was so powerful in the place. We shared about prior revivals in our area and as well as others throughout New York State (NYS) and Vermont.

I looked out and saw everyone worshiping in one accord, all with the same heart towards God. Michelle Adams and Heather Bartos led the praise and worship, which was outside of some people's boxes. They combined hymns with newer praise and worship songs. Even now, I find it hard to describe the scene. Everyone sang all the songs with the same passion and in unity, along with the angels in Heaven. No one was divided because of what they were used to in their own churches. It was glorious!

People told me afterwards that the moment that they walked through the door of the church they sensed the presence of God. That was what we wanted. That was what made all the difference …

people who were hungry and thirsty to be in His presence.

In our bulletin, we didn't list any titles next to the names of the 14 pastors and lay people who came prepared to share. They were asked in advance to pray about bringing a word, scripture, and/or prayer – whatever God had put on their hearts.

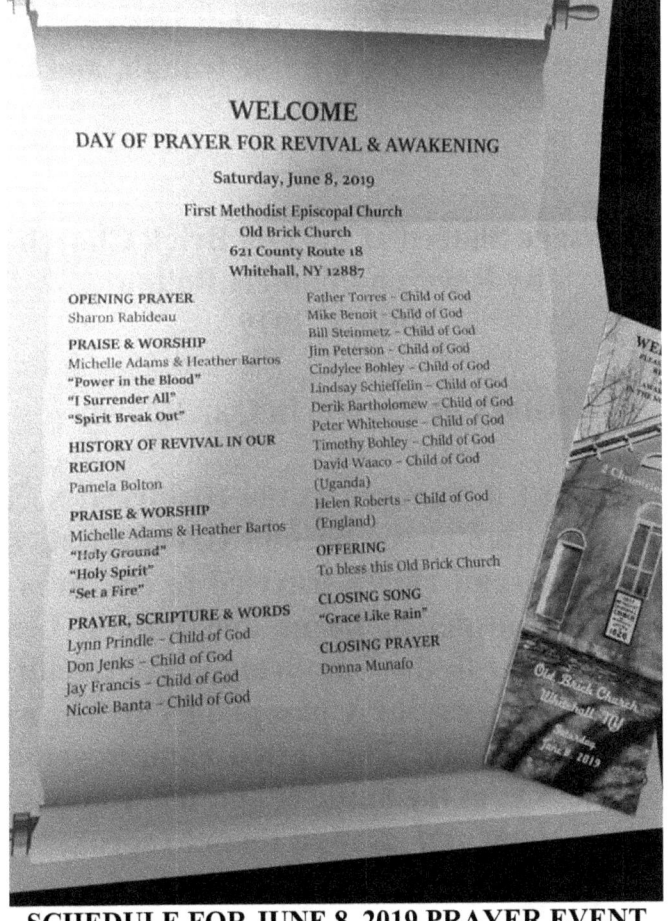

SCHEDULE FOR JUNE 8, 2019 PRAYER EVENT

In light of the fact that the church didn't have any electricity or water, we had prayed about how to do a baptism there on the property following the service. God made a way for us to borrow a horse trough from a local Amish family to do a baptism in. As Michelle Adams and I were leaving the church, we saw an Amish man walking on the side of the road. I told her to quickly stop the car and turn around. We pulled up and asked the man if he might have something that we could use to do a baptism at the special service that was coming up. He offered to let us use a horse trough, and it was perfect.

Message Shared at the Old Brick Church
By Reverend Pamela Bolton
June 8, 2019

History of Revival in Our Region

What I discovered at the Historical Society: During the time of the Second Great Awakening, Methodist circuit riders traveled to this area and shared the Gospel in barns and homes. Lemuel Smith was sent to the Cambridge, NY, circuit and Samuel Wigton to the Champlain Circuit, which included Whitehall. They often came together in Hampton, NY, at the home of Samuel Bibbons who welcomed them and allowed them to speak.

In 1791, Samuel Wigton preached in East Whitehall for the first time; and by 1796, there were 10 Methodists who organized themselves into a Methodist society under Reverend Lorenzo Dow. Services were first held in various homes, but later they met in a frame building (barn) on the property located just west of the church. Later on, services were held in a local schoolhouse.

The lives of the circuit riders were very difficult – arduous. I found the following information on the United Methodist Church.org website (www.umc.org).

Typically, circuit riders traveled 200 to 500 mile routes on horseback, and at times, they preached every day. Sometimes circuits were so large that it took six weeks to complete a cycle. Exhaustion, illness, animal attacks, and unfriendly encounters were constant threats.

Freeborn Garrettson (who oversaw the circuit riders in the Whitehall area) *said this, 'I was pursued by the wicked, knocked down, and left almost dead on the highway, my face scarred and bleeding and then imprisoned.'*

Days and nights were spent in the elements, hunting or fishing for food and depending on the hospitality of strangers.

Theirs was a difficult and often short life. Prior to 1847, nearly half of Methodist circuit riding preachers died before the age of 30. But their passion for saving souls was unprecedented, both then and now.

In the early 1800s, through the famous preaching of Reverend Kellogg, Whitehall became known an "evil and Godless place." At that time, the town was booming with many factories, and many activities were going on along the canal. It had many bars but not even a single church. But, there were some wise and Godly people who decided that a church needed to be built. So the first church, the Old Congregational Church, was built in what was then known as Skenesborough on the Burgoyne Road on the way to Castleton, VT.

In 1801, this area became part of the Brandon, VT, Circuit, which added a swing through the village of Whitehall. This circuit included Danby and Wells, VT, Granville with "Whitehell" and Crown Point, NY. [Used with permission from Brandon United Methodist Church web page (I suspect that the people who wrote this were familiar with the famous sermon by Reverend Kellogg.)] In 1817, in Brandon, a great revival prevailed in town; and about the first of September, 1835, a revival commenced and continued without interruption for some eight months.

In 1826, the Old Brick Church building was built for $1,600, and during the years to follow, it became the center for Christian services and preaching. There are reports of revivals and meetings at which this little church was filled to capacity. Throughout the years, the Old Brick Church has changed very little.

All across NYS as well as in other parts of the country, the revivals that took place when Charles Finney rode into a town were remarkable. He preached about repentance and putting one's trust in Jesus; and God used him powerfully to bring people into His Kingdom. Some historians called him the "Father of modern revivalism," and he paved the way for later revivalists like Dwight L. Moody, Billy Sunday, and Billy Graham.

He was known as a "Walking Revival" and a "God Quake." Wouldn't you like to be known as a "Walking Revival" every place that you set your feet?

Because of Finney's ministry: From January of 1826 through June 1831, Finney preached all over NYS and revival broke out. Many thousands of people became believers in Jesus during that time. There were parts of NYS that Finney termed "the burned-over districts," because spiritual awakening and revival had taken place so often in those areas that there were no more people left to witness to. For instance, in Oswego, there were reported to be at least 1,343 revivals between the years of 1825-1835.

Let's fast forward to 1876.... During the 100-year anniversary of our country and the time of the Third Great Awakening, there was a major revival that took place at the Old Brick Church in East Whitehall. The church held 250 people, but during the services, the church couldn't hold all the people who attended. Some had to sit outside and listen through open windows. Many people became believers in Jesus during that time.

I also found this Newspaper Clipping (1876?): The religious revival that has been going on at the First Baptist Church (in the village of Whitehall), under the guidance of C. C. Frost, has been fruitful of good works. Nearly two hundred people went forward and stayed for the inquiry meetings that were held after every service. The Baptist, Methodist, and Presbyterian societies worked shoulder to shoulder for two weeks of services. This is quoted as being "one of the greatest religious revivals witnessed in this place."

In an article in *The Whitehall Times* from March 30, 1978 entitled, "The Whitehall Temperance Club–1876" (by Doris B. Morton, Town Historian), it was reported: "During the year 1876, a great revival movement swept Whitehall. All the churches held meetings and reported the many people who reformed as a result of the movement. This was true in neighboring communities as well. Speakers were imported to add to the work of the local clergy."

There was another article from 1878 that was found in an old scrapbook that read, "The religious revival is not at all in the wane at this place. Meetings are held during the week at the Presbyterian and Baptist Churches. At each of these places there is great awakening."

In 1883, revival broke out again at the Old Brick Church, and 40 more souls were saved; and in 1885, Rev. Joseph Zweifel ministered throughout the winter at the First Baptist Church, and 100 people became believers.

I'm sure that those believers were praying for generations that were yet to come, praying for us. I believe that God was answering their prayers as we met to pray for our local community as well as the whole Northeast on Saturday, June 8, 2019.

T. L. Osborn

Some of you may be familiar with the famous evangelist, T. L. Osborn. Well, in 1904, another famous evangelist, T. H. Osborn (possibly an older relative of T. L Osborn), was brought to Whitehall by the village Methodist Episcopal Church for two weeks of revival services. There was a service every evening except on Saturdays.

The following was what I was able to find out about this evangelist:
Copied from Historic Lebanon, Ohio, Facebook Page

The Western Star June 18, 1903:
"SPECIAL MEETING:

EVANGELIST T. H. OSBORN of Chicago... He is a fine speaker and singer and has marked success all over the North, having held meetings in some of our largest cities.... Bring a silver collection to help pay car fare and other expenses.

NOTE: Theodore Hollingsworth Osborn (1851-1932)

Osborn was known as "the Drummer Evangelist" and spent much of the late 19th century and early 20th century conducting religion revivals all over the country. They were usually in Methodist Episcopal Churches and often lasted for weeks. His religious exploits and successes were often mentioned in such periodicals as *The Christian Advocate* and *Christian Workers Magazine*. The August 18, 1897 issue of the Northwest Christian Advocate in Chicago stated, "Zeal, tact, and power characterize his work."

In 1991, the local Catholic Church hosted an Ecumenical prayer and hymn sing service, and other pastors from the area took part in the meeting. It was the third service in a series of meetings planned by the clergy of Whitehall. At this time in Whitehall, there were also many other special services where people gathered together to worship and pray. This was just after the height of the Catholic Charismatic movement.

We can be encouraged by the fortitude and determination of the people of God who plowed the ground in our area as well as all across NYS. We must get out of our comfort zones, out of the four walls of our churches, and go out and reach the people. Don't think that it will always be comfortable; it wasn't always comfortable for the twelve disciples (most of whom laid down their lives for the sake of the Gospel), and it wasn't always comfortable for the circuit riders either. Jesus never said it would be comfortable, but He did give us the Great Commission which says:

And Jesus came and spoke to them, saying, "All authority has been given to Me in heaven and on earth. Go therefore and make disciples of all the nations, baptizing them in the name of the Father and of the Son and of the Holy Spirit, teaching them to observe all things that I have commanded you; and lo, I am with you always, even to the end of the age." Amen. Matthew 28:18-20 (NKJV)

My heart's desire it to spur you on to ACTION. It isn't enough to just believe it; we need to act on it. There are those for whom life and death hang in the balance. We believe that we are living in a season where there is great opportunity to minister to people in our local communities. There are many who are hurting, and they are just waiting for us to talk to them, to share the Good News of Jesus Christ. It doesn't have to be complicated or awkward. We don't have to be weird! We can just share the story of what Jesus has done in our own lives.

So, I ask you this: "What about God has changed from the late 1700s, the 1800s, and early 1900s?" The Bible says, "Jesus Christ is the same yesterday, today, and forever." (Hebrews 13:8) If this is true, and it is; then I want to ask you again: "Why not you? Why not right now in your community?"

I want to encourage each one of you to find out the history of what God has done in your city or town in days gone by. Stand on the Word of God, and believe that He wants to move in power again but in even greater measure than He has in the past.

I love what Charles Finney said. "Revival is a renewed conviction of sin and repentance, followed by an intense desire to live in obedience to God. It is giving up one's will to God in deep humility."

Information above was taken from the following unless otherwise noted:

Whitehall Times articles written by Doris A. Morton and compiled by Carol Greenough; newspaper clippings, scrap books, and misc. articles owned by the Historical Society of Whitehall; and Christian History Institute – online.

God had directed me to bring His people together in unity to seek His face and to pray that He would move in power once again in our region. We began to pray earnestly, in one accord, for full-blown revival and awakening along the NY/VT border. God heard our prayers, and look what He has done!

We are so very blessed to see with our own eyes, from the planet, some of the answers to the prayers that we and others have prayed.

Our dear friend, Nicole Banta, who was a missionary to Colombia for one year, went to IRIS Global Harvest School # 37, in 2022. At the time that she was attending, there was a civil war going on in Mozambique, so the students traveled to Israel, then on to South Africa where they went to Mbombela, East London, and the Republic of Transkei, as they were taking their classes. There was a bag of stakes that the leaders had that had been prayed over by multiple leaders over a long period of time. When the students finished up the school, they were each given two yellow tent stakes and tasked with planting them in territory they wanted to claim for the Lord. Nicole called me up and told me that she felt that God wanted her to put one of the stakes in Whitehall, and I was thrilled, because I had been believing God for great things to happen there for years. It was on January 4, 2023, that we climbed up on the icy mountainside behind Skene Manor and planted the stake. Then we prayed and thanked God for what He was going to do in this community.

In 2019, I published my first book about revival and awakening, *Ushering in Revival and Awakening – Fanning the Flames of Revival*. God inspired me to continue writing books, five more that were all relating to revival and awakening in some way. I believe that He put it in my heart to dig up the old wells of revival in our area and pray for fresh living water and to encourage the people of God to believe Him for more today.

MISSIONARY NICOLE BANTA AND PASTOR PAMELA BOLTON - STAKE WAS PLACED ABOVE WHITEHALL JANUARY 4, 2023

Don't think for one minute that the devil didn't try to come in and disrupt the plans of God. He tried several means to accomplish this, but God's will was completed anyway. Never give in to the devil or his schemes to keep you from your purpose.

When some of those that God called to work with me rejected the call, God was still faithful, and His will was accomplished anyway.

Over the past six years (with COVID and other challenges), I have learned that no matter what... Be faithful and keep moving forward, because God is always faithful to keep His Word. We may not see the answers to our prayers in our timing, but we'll certainly see them in His timing; and sometimes His timing is while we're still here on the earth.

A PIVOTAL MOMENT

I met Bishop Lance Johnson in the summer of 2023 at Kingsway Worship Center in Hudson Falls, NY. I asked him to come and minister at Out of the Box Worship Center and other area churches. He said that he would get a hold of me during the fall of that year. I didn't hear from him, so I sent him a gentle reminder by text on January 9, 2024. He responded immediately and asked to talk by phone that day. He said that the Lord had been speaking to him about this area and that he felt God was telling him to make himself available as much as possible to our region. That day, we scheduled two separate weeks of meetings for the coming summer, one in June and the other in August. In June, Bishop asked me if I would help him organize a crusade in our area. I didn't need to pray about it, because I had already prayed, and I immediately knew that this was part of the answer to my prayers as well as the prayers of many others.

During Lance's June trip, he had already asked Pastors Jason and Tammie LaPierre to help with organizing the Crusade, and then he also asked Pastors Tim and Cindylee Bohley to join the team.

In August of 2024, we called an initial, small pastors' meeting with pastors and leaders from the surrounding area, both from New York and Vermont. In October 2024, we followed up with a much larger meeting, and many more pastors and leaders of churches and ministries along the NY/VT border got on board after Bishop Lance shared his vision for the Crusade. He came up this way again for another meeting in the March of 2025. By that time, we had approximately 30 churches and ministries committed to being a part of the Crusade.

AUGUST 26, 2024 - FIRST CRUSADE PLANNING MEETING
[MISSING FROM PHOTO: FATHER LEO BENJAMIN (PHOTOGRAPHER), SCHUYLER SCHIEFFELIN, AMY ROBBINS, AND JENNIFER BROOKS]

Many individuals and churches committed to praying for the upcoming Crusade. Some people prayed faithfully, daily, and some groups met once a week to seek the Lord for an outpouring of His Spirit in our area once again.

During the fall of 2024, we began to pray approximately once a week at our home; and then in the early spring of 2025, we moved the prayer to our humble Out of the Box Worship Center storefront. As the dates of the Crusade approached, we began to pray at the Skenesborough Amphitheater once a week.

Our friend and mentor, Dean Braxton, came to NY and VT the week before the Crusade began. He had been scheduled in for that week prior to the planning of the Crusade. Some would say that this was a coincidence, but I believe that it was a divine assignment. Dean actively helped to promote the Crusade at each service that he spoke at as well as in interviews with Father Leo Benjamin.

I am so thankful to God that between July 17 and 20, He drew hundreds of His people together to worship Him with one heart and one mind, and He also drew many unbelievers in. Over 200 people came to know Jesus as Lord and Savior over the course of the four days of the Crusade, and many recommitted theirs lives to Him as well. There were many baptisms that took place, too. We are so very grateful to God for all that he began in our area at the Awake America Crusade and for Bishop Lance's part in making it happen, and we believe that this is just the beginning of what God is going to do in this region.

We have planned continuing Crusade meetings once a month, and at the first one that was held at Calvary Life Center in Glens Falls on Friday, August 1, 2025, God again moved in power. Many people were either saved or recommitted their lives to the Lord, and others were set free from longstanding issues like addiction, anxiety, and depression, which held them back from walking in the fullness of all that God has for them.

Chapter 2

Preparation, News Articles, and Advertising

GETTING READY...
A CALL TO BE INVOLVED
PROPHETIC WORD ABOUT THE CRUSADE
By Prophet Bill Emmons
May 2025

"As I was teaching a weekly Bible study prior to the Crusade, I began to mention about the importance of pastors getting on board. I mentioned that God had tried to move in the city of Albany about 10 years earlier at Pastor Charlie and Tammy Muller's church. I had spoken a prophetic word about it the year before it happened. However, Albany pastors did not join in when the revival broke out, and the Lord gave me a word at that time that He only moves where there's unity so the revival ended.

"I then saw an image of Bishop Lance Johnson preaching in the amphitheater in Whitehall and seeds of fire were flowing out of his mouth into the hearts of the people and into the region. The Lord said that it was not the fullness of the revival, but Lance had come to plant seeds (a seedbed) of revival and fire in the northeast for what was to come."

It is crucial that as this move of God moves forward, that pastors and leaders walk in love and unity with one another!

10,000 CRUSADE POSTCARDS
FRONT

BACK

**ADVERTISING FOR PASTORS' AND LEADERS' MEETING
SATURDAY, MARCH 15, 2025**

BANNER AT OUT OF THE BOX WORSHIP CENTER STOREFRONT

**The following article was written by:
Pastor Leo Benjamin
Founder of *MyFaithNews*
Article Date: October 16, 2024**

Get ready for a powerful move of God as Awake America Crusade 2025 returns to Whitehall, New York, bringing a revival that is set to transform the region. This highly anticipated event will be held at the Skenesborough Park Amphitheater from Thursday, July 17th to Sunday, July 20th, 2025, with services starting at 6:30 p.m. nightly.

Bishop Lance Johnson of Lance Johnson Ministries, in partnership with Pastor Jason LaPierre, Pastor Timothy Bohley, and Pastor Pamela Bolton, will host this revival. It will gather close to 100 pastors from the region and beyond, united in faith, to ignite hearts and inspire lives.

OLD PHOTO OF BAPTISM IN THE MIDDLE OF WINTER

Awake America Revival 2025 Details

- **Event:** Awake America Crusade 2025
- **Location:** Skenesborough Park, Amphitheater, Skenesborough Drive, Whitehall, NY 12887
- **Dates:** Thursday, July 17 – Sunday, July 20, 2025
- **Time:** 6:30 p.m. Nightly
- **Hosted By:** Bishop Lance Johnson, Pastor Jason LaPierre, Pastor Timothy Bohley, and Pastor Pamela Bolton

As we look ahead to this exciting Crusade, we also reflect on the spiritual history of the region, where the wells of faith were first opened. One of the most significant events took place more than 150 years ago along the banks of the Battenkill River. This revival story, which involves a courageous baptismal ceremony in the dead of winter, serves as a reminder of God's enduring power to transform lives.

Historical Revival in Washington County

In January 1843, a powerful revival broke out in the Greenwich, NY area. Elder Arthur, father of future President Chester A. Arthur, led a baptismal ceremony in the freezing waters of the Battenkill River. Despite the freezing conditions, 50 people were baptized, with an additional 20 joining later, totaling 70 baptisms on that frigid day. The revival continued, and by the next Sunday, 35 more people were baptized, bringing the total to 105 baptisms during that revival.

This remarkable moment in history reflects the perseverance of faith in the region, even under the harshest conditions. Elder Arthur's endurance in leading the baptisms was seen as a miracle, one that speaks to the power of God working through willing vessels to bring transformation.

Revival Today: A Legacy of Faith

Just as the Battenkill River carried those believers into a renewed life in Christ, we believe the Awake America Crusade 2025 will stir up a fresh outpouring of faith. The same spirit of revival that touched lives in Greenwich, Cambridge, and White Creek more than a century ago is ready to move again in Whitehall, NY. This event will rekindle the spiritual wells of the region, and the presence of God will bring transformation, healing, and breakthrough.

Why You Should Attend Awake America Crusade 2025

If you're searching for a fresh encounter with God, deeper spiritual renewal, or a new sense of purpose, this event is for you. Join us at the Skenesborough Park Amphitheater to experience powerful worship, life-changing messages, and a community of believers seeking revival.

Don't miss this historic event! The Awake America Crusade 2025 is an opportunity for families, individuals, and churches to come together and witness the move of God in Whitehall, NY. This event is for everyone—whether you're new to the faith or have been walking with the Lord for years.

Mark your calendars for July 17th-20th, 2025, and be part of a Crusade that will leave a lasting impact on the region. The wells of revival are opening, and the time to step into the future is now!

Join the Conversation

Stay up to date with Awake America Crusade 2025 by following Lance Johnson Ministries and partnering churches on social media. Use the hashtag #AwakeAmerica2025 to share your experiences, connect with other attendees, and spread the word about this exciting Crusade.

Make plans now to be part of Awake America Crusade 2025 in Whitehall, NY—a revival event that will stir your faith, renew your spirit, and set your heart on fire for the Gospel!

Event Information Recap

- **What:** Awake America Crusade 2025
- **Where:** Skenesborough Park, Amphitheater, Skenesborough Drive, Whitehall, NY 12887
- **When:** July 17-20, 2025 | 6:30 p.m. Nightly
- **Sponsored by:** Lance Johnson Ministries

Don't miss this opportunity to be part of an unforgettable experience!

By blending the legacy of past revivals with the excitement of today's movement, Awake America Crusade 2025 promises to be an event that will change lives and revive the spirit of the region.

The author is the pastor of the Church of the Crucified One in Moretown, Vermont, and the publisher of *MyFaithNews*.

Igniting Revival Across the Adirondacks, The Capital Region & Vermont, July 2025

Article Date: November 4, 2024
By Pastor Leo Benjamin *MyFaithNews*
Used with permission.

BISHOP LANCE JOHNSON

On Monday, October 28, pastors and faith leaders from across the Adirondacks to the Capital Region, including Vermont, gathered in Whitehall, New York, for a pivotal planning meeting focused on bringing a major revival to the area. The "Awake America Crusade," scheduled for July 17-20, 2025, aims to unite people for four nights of worship, inspiration, and transformation. Hosted at the scenic

Skenesborough Amphitheater on Skenesborough Drive, Whitehall, NY 12887, the crusade promises a revival experience designed to unify believers, introduce seekers to faith, and strengthen the bonds of community across upstate New York, Vermont, and beyond. Sponsored by Lance Johnson Ministries in partnership with Pastor Jason LaPierre, Pastor Timothy Bohley, and Pastor Pamela Bolton, the meeting laid a foundation for strategic planning, rallying churches, and ensuring the event will deliver an impactful message to all who attend. In the words of Bishop Lance Johnson, "True revival isn't about the numbers; it's about lives being changed. It's about igniting a passion for God and a compassion for people."

PASTORS AND LEADERS GATHERING TO WORSHIP AND PRAY IN PREPARATIOIN FOR THE CRUSADE

Uniting Churches From the Adirondacks to the Capital Region & Vermont for Revival

The October 28 meeting set the tone for unity, with a focus on building collaboration among regional churches to make the crusade successful. Organizers encouraged pastors and church leaders to mobilize their congregations, sharing the vision of the crusade and encouraging members to attend, volunteer, and pray.

Pastor Jason LaPierre, one of the crusade's organizers, emphasized the importance of a united effort, stating, "If we truly want to see a move of God, we need to come together as one. This crusade is a chance for our churches to set aside differences and work side by side to impact lives." Leaders at the meeting discussed organizing teams for setup, prayer support, hospitality, and outreach, ensuring a welcoming experience for everyone who attends.

Strategies for Reaching the Region and Beyond

A major topic of discussion was how to reach not only churchgoers but also those who may feel disconnected from faith. The leaders explored promotional strategies, including using digital platforms, social media, local media, and community events to generate awareness and build excitement leading up to the crusade.

The event's unique message is one of hope and renewal, with Bishop Johnson highlighting, "There's a hunger in people's hearts, whether they realize it or not. The Awake America Crusade is about answering that hunger with the love of God and the truth of the Gospel." This call to reach those seeking meaning and purpose will guide outreach efforts, as organizers work to ensure the message of revival reaches all corners of the Region and beyond.

The Power of Worship and Message in an Inspiring Setting

The Skenesborough Amphitheater offers a picturesque and open-air environment for worship and community connection. Each night of the crusade, beginning at 6:30 p.m., attendees will experience live worship music, drawing hearts together in a spirit of unity and reverence. Music will include a blend of traditional hymns and contemporary praise, creating an atmosphere where generations can worship together.

Following worship, Bishop Lance Johnson will deliver messages centered on hope, renewal, and faith. Each sermon will emphasize life transformation, encouraging attendees to move beyond past struggles and embrace a path toward spiritual growth and fulfillment. With contributions from a diverse lineup of church leaders, His messages will resonate with people from all walks of life, presenting timeless truths in a way that connects with modern-day challenges.

Building Excitement for the Awake America Crusade in July 2025

The planning meeting on October 28th laid the groundwork for what organizers and pastors hope will be a transformative experience for the Region. The Awake America Crusade is more than just an event; it's a vision for revival that reaches beyond church walls to impact entire communities. With plans in motion, pastors are now calling on their congregations and communities to join them in anticipation, prayer, and preparation for what God will do.

As Bishop Lance Johnson expressed, "We serve a God of miracles, and when we come together in faith, there's no limit to what He can do. This crusade is about lifting up Jesus and letting His love change lives." This spirit of expectancy resonated throughout the meeting, as each leader committed to playing a role in making the Awake America Crusade a powerful moment of revival.

The event will take place at Skenesborough Amphitheater on Skenesborough Drive, Whitehall, NY, from July 17-20, 2025, with services starting at 6:30 p.m. each night. Churches, community members, and people from all backgrounds are invited to attend, bring friends and family, and experience God in a way that will be life-changing.

A Call to Prayer and Unity for a Revival Movement

For many attendees of the planning meeting, the Awake America Crusade represents a historic moment for the Region, where believers and seekers alike can come together to encounter God. The message of unity and transformation extends an invitation to every person in the community to participate—whether by attending, volunteering, praying, or helping to spread the word.

Organizers and church leaders are already seeing the potential for a spiritual awakening that can bring hope, healing, and purpose to those who attend. They are calling on all who believe in the power of prayer and community to support the crusade's success through active involvement.

Mark your calendar for July 17-20, 2025, and prepare to witness the power of revival at Skenesborough Amphitheater. Together, we're standing in faith, preparing for the Move of the

Holy Spirit, and looking forward to a transformative experience that only Jesus can offer to the people of upstate New York and Vermont, lifting the Region and beyond.

The author is the pastor of the Church of the Crucified One in Moretown, Vermont, and the publisher of *MyFaithNews*. **Used with permission.**

Join Us in Prayer for Full-blown Revival and Awakening Along the NY/VT Border Awake America Crusade

Co-Authored by Pastor Pamela Bolton, Out of the Box Worship Center, and Pastor Leo Benjamin, *MyFaithNews*
Article Date: January 1, 2025

Skenesborough Park Amphitheater, Whitehall, NY
July 17-20, 2025

A Call to Revival and Awakening

For generations, New York and Vermont have witnessed powerful moves of God—times of deep spiritual renewal that transformed communities, saved lives, and ignited faith across the region. Today, the same Spirit of revival is stirring hearts.

The Awake America Crusade is a call to believers everywhere to pray fervently and unite for a fresh outpouring of God's Spirit. This four-day event will bring together pastors, leaders, and believers from across the region to seek God's presence and believe for revival that changes our time.

Historical Context: Revivals That Changed the Region

Our region's rich spiritual heritage inspires us today. Here are highlights of significant revivals that shaped our communities and brought thousands to faith in Jesus Christ:

In the mid-19th century, Vermont was a focal point of spiritual awakening. The revival of 1858 swept across the western border towns, marked by extraordinary conversions that transcended social and economic barriers.

"The work is so general and remarkable as to attract the attention of all classes. It is not confined to the churches; hundreds are converted at prayer meetings, in private houses, in the workshops, and at their work in the fields."
(***The Troy Weekly Times***, **April 3, 1858**)

This revival reached men and women from all walks of life—lawyers, physicians, tradesmen, farmers, and laborers. It demonstrated the power of the Gospel to unite and transform entire communities.

1906: Ticonderoga, NY—A Blaze of Glory

In the early 20th century, Ticonderoga became the epicenter of an evangelical campaign that saw unprecedented spiritual awakening. Over 825 conversions were recorded during the meetings, which packed tents and churches beyond capacity.

"Never in Ticonderoga, and possibly never in Northern New York, has such a great spiritual quickening been experienced. The campaign closed in a blaze of glory."
(Evangelical Campaign Report)

What set this revival apart was the diversity of those impacted—people from all creeds, professions, and ages made public commitments to Christ. Beyond conversions, the revival stirred a renewed civic conscience and commitment to moral and spiritual ideals.

1915: Granville, NY—The Big Tabernacle Revival

Granville witnessed a historic revival under Evangelist H.D. Sheldon. The meetings were held in a massive tabernacle, accommodating over 1,500 attendees. These gatherings became a hub of spiritual renewal.

"The speaker held his audience in rapt attention, and the intense interest in his message promises great times of spiritual renewal."
(***The Granville Sentinel***, **November 19, 1915**)

Over the course of five weeks, these meetings united churches, families, and individuals. Many found salvation and a spiritual home, while others experienced personal and community transformation.

1880: Howes Cave, NY
Camp Meetings That Shaped a Generation

The camp meetings of Howes Cave drew thousands—some traveling over 100 miles by horse-drawn carriage. These gatherings became a beacon of spiritual devotion.

"Thousands crowded around the preacher's stand to eagerly drink in the Gospel truths presented. The woods literally swarmed with life."
(***The Cobleskill Index**,* **August 26, 1880**)

Despite the challenges of dust, heat, and travel, people came with hearts hungry for the Word of God. Preachers like Rev. Mr. Thompson of Canajoharie and Rev. Mr. Ford of Schenectady delivered sermons that resonated deeply, leaving a lasting spiritual impact.

A Modern Cry for Revival

These moments in history demonstrate the incredible impact of revival on individuals, families, and entire communities. They remind us of what God can do when His people unite in faith and prayer.

In the same spirit, we are calling on believers to gather for the Awake America Crusade. Let's pray together for revival and awakening that surpasses anything we have seen in our lifetime.

Event Details

Dates: July 17–20, 2025

Location: Skenesborough Park Amphitheater, Whitehall, NY

This event is being led by Bishop Lance Johnson, Pastors Jason and Tammie LaPierre, Pastors Tim and Cindylee Bohley, and Pastor Pamela Bolton. Together with local leaders and churches, we are believing God for a mighty move of His Spirit.

Pray With Us and Take Part

How You Can Pray:

- **Pray for Revival:** That hearts will be softened and lives transformed.

- **Pray for Unity:** That believers across denominations will join together.

- **Pray for Transformation:** That this Crusade will leave a lasting legacy of faith.

Why Not Here? Why Not Now?

The testimonies of the past inspire us to believe for a greater move of God today. As we approach the Awake America Crusade, let's join together in faith and prayer, expecting miracles and transformation.

Let's declare together:

Why not you? Why not me? Why not right here, right now?

Co-Authored by Pastor Pamela Bolton, Out of the Box Worship Center & First Baptist Church, Whitehall, and Pastor Leo Benjamin, *MyFaithNews,* **Used with permission.**

Revival Awakening in the Northeast: Whitehall, NY Prepares for a Transformative Crusade

By Pastor Leo Benjamin *MyFaithNews*, A Historic Move of God, the Whitehall NY Revival 2025 is set to inspire many.

Whitehall, NY – March 15, 2025

A powerful movement of revival is taking shape in Upstate New York and Vermont as churches and leaders prepare for the highly anticipated Awake America Crusade, scheduled for July 17-20, 2025, at the Skenesborough Amphitheater in Whitehall, NY. With over 1,000 attendees expected, this four-night event is being led by Bishop Lance Johnson of Lance Johnson Ministries, alongside Pastors Jason & Tammie LaPierre, Pastors Timothy & Cindylee Bohley, and Pastor Pamela Bolton. This crusade is more than just an event;

it is a call to the great commission to bring salvation, restoration, and revival to the region.

A Call to Revival and Unity

On March 15, 2025, pastors and Christian leaders from across the region gathered at First Baptist Church of Whitehall for a powerful planning meeting, unified by a shared vision for revival. Bishop Lance Johnson set the tone for the gathering with fervent prayer, calling upon the Holy Spirit to move mightily among them. As worship filled the room, hearts were stirred, and a deep sense of expectancy arose for the outpouring of God's presence.

WORSHIP TEAM: Heather Bartos and Derik Bartholomew

"If we want to see a move of God, it starts here and now. We must break free from routine, from unbelief, and cry out with hunger for more of Him," Johnson declared passionately.

He emphasized that revival is not confined to a single event—it must be birthed within the hearts of believers long before any gathering takes place. Johnson challenged churches to prioritize prayer and unity, urging them to move beyond routine programs and embrace the power of intercession. He reminded those present that revival is not about numbers, but about transformation—of lives, churches, and entire communities.

Bishop Lance addressing regional pastors and leaders

With the Northeast ripe for a spiritual awakening, the meeting concluded with leaders committing to a season of fervent prayer, preparing the way for a great move of God at the Awake America Great Crusade 2025.

Worship at the leadership meeting

A Burden for the Lost: Igniting Evangelism

A major theme of the meeting was the urgency of evangelism and the burden for the lost. Johnson shared his personal testimony of radical transformation, underscoring the power of persistent prayer.

"I owe the thousands of souls I've ministered to, to my brother who never stopped praying for me when I was lost," Bishop Lance shared.

Mobilizing Churches

This crusade will only be successful if churches mobilize and believers take action. Pastor Jason and Pastor Tammy LaPierre will lead the altar ministry team, ensuring that trained individuals are equipped to lead people to Christ.

Altar Ministry Training Dates:
• Faith Chapel in Whitehall is on Friday, April 4 at 6:30 PM.
• Kingsway Worship Center is on Friday, May 2 at 6:30 PM.

Additionally, Pastor Bill and Lisa Harrington are heading up the ushers, greeters, and parking attendants' ministry, ensuring the event runs smoothly. Churches are strongly encouraged to set up booths at the event, offering ministry resources and discipleship opportunities for new believers.

"We need every church involved—this is not about competition but about uniting the Body of Christ," Johnson emphasized.

A Vision for Lasting Impact: More Than a Crusade

While the crusade will be a powerful four-night gathering, its ultimate goal is to spark a movement that will continue for years to come. Leaders were urged to break free from denominational barriers and unite under one purpose: the advancement of the Kingdom of God.

The meeting began with intense prayer and intercession as leaders stood together, believing for revival in Upstate New York and Vermont.

"Revival doesn't begin with a crusade. It begins in our hearts, our homes, and our churches long before the event itself," Johnson reminded.

How You Can Get Involved

The Awake America Crusade is set to be a landmark event for the Northeast. Churches and individuals are encouraged to take part, volunteer, and pray for a mighty move of God.

The author, Leo Benjamin, is the pastor of the Church of the Crucified One in Moretown, Vermont, and the publisher of *MyFaithNews*, Used with permission.

Awake America Crusade to bring four nights of revival to Whitehall

WHITEHALL – The Awake America Crusade, a four-night Christian revival event, will be held at the Skenesborough Amphitheater Thursday through Sunday, July 17-20, beginning each evening at 6:30 PM.

The event is part of a nationwide crusade led by Bishop Lance Johnson of Relevate Church in Ranger, Georgia, who is holding 26 revival gatherings across the country this year.

Johnson has been involved in sustained revivals in Georgia and Kentucky in recent years.

Contributed Photo

The Whitehall crusade has drawn support form pastors across the region, spanning from areas south of Albany to Northern Vermont, with hopes of making a lasting spiritual impact on the local community.

Each evening will feature live praise and worship music, followed by a message from Bishop Johnson. Organizers invite all individuals and families to attend, especially those seeking healing, encouragement, or renewal.

The event is free and open to the public.

For more information, visit:
www.facebook.com/groups/UpstateNYMinistryNetwork/events.
www.nyvtmedia.com, *Sentinel Times*,
Thursday, July 17, 2025, Used with permission.

PRE-CRUSADE PRAYER MEETING AT SKENESBOROUGH AMPHITHEATER WITH PASTOR DERIK BARTHOLOMEW

PRE-CRUSADE PRAYER MEETING AT SKENESBOROUGH AMPHITHEATER WITH REVEREND DONNA LaPIERRE

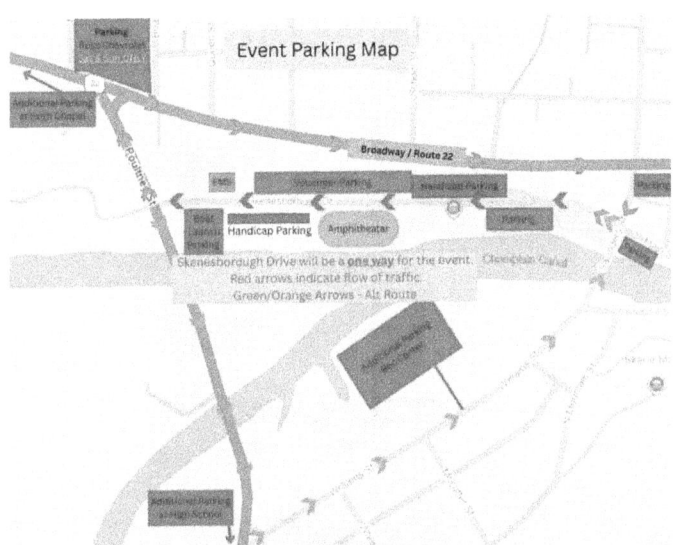

MAP CREATED BY PASTOR BILL HARRINGTON

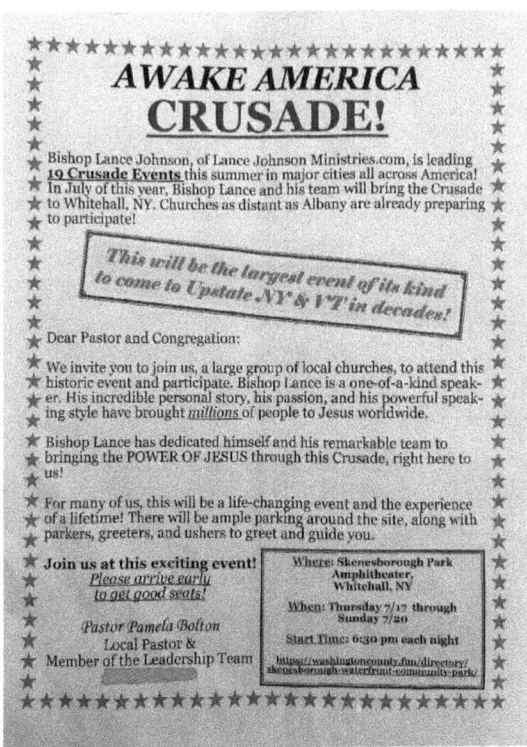

FLYER CREATED BY LINDSAY SCHIEFFELIN

THERE IS MORE TO COME….

MONTHLY CRUSADE SCHEDULE

CALVARY ASSEMBLY OF GOD
100 Sherman Avenue
Glens Falls, NY
FRIDAY, AUGUST 1, 6:30 PM

FIRST BAPTIST CHURCH
41 Williams Street
Whitehall, NY
FRIDAY, SEPTEMBER 5, 6:30 PM

GRANVILLE BAPTIST CHURCH
23 Quaker Street
Granville, NY
FRIDAY, OCTOBER 3, 6:30 PM

JACOB'S WELL FELLOWSHIP
29 W. Main Street
Cambridge, NY
FRIDAY, NOVEMBER 7, 6:30 PM

If my people, which are called by my name, shall humble themselves, and pray, and seek my face, and turn from their wicked ways; then will I hear from heaven, and will forgive their sin, and will heal their land.
2 Chronicles 7:14

Chapter 3

Bishop Lance Johnson's Account

"My personal account of the
Awake America Crusade
July 17-20, 2025

"From the moment God breathed the inspiration for the Crusade in Upstate New York, I experienced His favor and grace upon every effort toward it. I believe this favor and grace was the result of countless prayers made by generations past as well as from many in the region that are hungry for the presence and glory of God.

"The first miracle we saw was the unity God brought between so many churches and their leaders. Everyone seemed to come together to pray and serve as one body with no one promoting anything except Jesus and a hunger for more of Him.

"The presence of the Lord was literally tangible, and the conviction of the Holy Spirit was in every service to draw the lost to salvation, to woo the prodigal's home, and draw the believer ever closer to Himself. Every worship service was filled with a hunger that resulted in the highest praise and the most intimate of worship. You could see the joy on the faces of the people as they exalted the Lord in praise, and you could see the tears that ran down their faces when His presence would come upon the people like cascading waves during worship.

"My mind will be forever be filled with the memories of what I experienced and what I saw God do among His people. At every altar call, the Lord's presence would draw people with such fervency that it seemed impossible to escape. People flooded the altars every night, weeping and calling upon the Lord in repentance, seeking to receive salvation and restoration. People from every walk of life came and gave their hearts to the Lord, from those bound by addiction to people that had served in ministry but had never been truly born again. You could literally see the transformation come upon people as they cried and prayed in the altars, and the testimonies flowed from many who experienced the life-changing power of God.

"Every single service was powerful and unique, but the last night stands out as God seemed to literally set down on His people. Spontaneous worship broke out and people worshipped with such intensity and intimacy that the sound that rose from the place sounded more heavenly than earthly. It's as if heaven and the angels joined in the worship and the sound that came forth is something I will never be able to forget. I remember looking up at one point during this intense worship, and most of the worship team was either on their knees or face down on the floor.

"At one-point spontaneous prayer and intercession broke out, and it seemed as if it would never stop. Several people were on the floor on their faces while others wept, but it seemed that every voice was crying out to God in one mind with one voice; and the only way I can describe it is to say heaven and earth collided.

"I believe these services are just the beginning of a true awakening that God has instituted among His people, and if the people will remain hungry, humble, and broken before the Lord, it will continue and even spread throughout our nation and even the world. It would be very difficult to go back to church as usual after experiencing such a mighty out pouring of God's Spirit. It has created a deep hunger for the more of God and a determined desire to host His presence over doing church as usual.

Bishop Lance Johnson
Relevate Church, Ranger, GA

Chapter 4

Revival Stories

Look What The Lord Has Done!

Only the Beginning...

On the first night of the Crusade, it was extremely hot in the sanctuary at First Baptist Church in Whitehall, NY. At the last minute, we had to hold the meeting indoors because of the weather. People began arriving early, and the place swelled to capacity with approximately 300 individuals in attendance. Everyone packed into that church, and there were people standing outside as well as some sitting on the front steps. There was great excitement in the air about what God was going to over the four-day Crusade. The presence of the Lord was strong, and people gathered in unity from numerous regional churches.

Nights two and three were held at the Skenesborough Amphitheater, and approximately 300 people attended each evening. On night three, we were blessed to have people from Georgia there with an outdoor baptistry, and many people were baptized.

Night four was held at the Granville Baptist Church due to inclement weather. That last night, God came and moved among His people in a very special and powerful way. The Glory of God filled the church. It reminded me of when the priests couldn't stand to minister at the dedication of Solomon's temple in the Bible (2 Chronicles 5:13-14). The musicians stopped playing, and Bishop Lance was quiet. He didn't want to touch what God was doing. We had a moment of visitation from the Lord. It was real! It was powerful! It was life-changing! I suspect that many of the people who were in attendance that evening will never be the same again.

The Gathering of the Lions Meetings (meetings with area pastors and leaders) were held both Friday and Saturday mornings at the Granville Baptist Church, and they were very powerful as well. The presence of the Lord was strong in every service that was part of the Crusade week. I thank God for meeting us in a very real and special way.

I want to let you read, in people's own words, what God did in their lives during the crusade. God met each person in an individual and unique way as He always does. He is always touching those who are touching Him, and many who were there came hungry and desiring more of God.

This move of God just getting started....

"Good morning, I can't thank you enough for your obedience and vision. The last night transformed my heart. I am not the same anymore."

Roberto Cabrera

"Just had to express, I can't keep it inside!

"I know there has been a spiritual warfare that has been going on in my life. This Crusade, God showed up to remind me that it's all about Him... to open my heart to its fullest capacity and let the Holy Spirit reign on the inside that the

outside of me must fully worship and honor God no matter what the world might think!

"That heaven will come down, if we are all in one accord, and bless almost everyone present!

"What a special sweet anointing!"
Bruce Turco

From January to April 2025, we had experienced personal revival and mountaintop experiences that led us to receiving clear direction and assignment from God to what He wanted us to do in Vermont, after moving us here from Canada.

Shortly after returning from a wonderful family vacation in early July, the enemy started attacking us relentlessly on many fronts. By the time the Crusade in Whitehall, NY on July 17th with Bishop Lance Johnson started, we were in disarray and in need of fire.

As soon as we stepped into the packed-out Baptist church on the first night, our hearts were invaded by the Holy Spirit and His Love, along with a powerful presence of Unity in the Body of Christ. We were strengthened almost immediately.

For the next three nights we experienced and witnessed personal revival breaking out in those around us and in our own hearts. We came away with many new divine connections and a greater sense of the unity in the local body.

It has confirmed and ignited the fire in our hearts once again for the direction God is leading us. We are excited and looking forward to being part of what God is doing in the Northeast region that was started before this Crusade ever began, through the prayers of the faithful for revival in the region.
Michael and Elsie Perry

"I have always believed that Jesus Christ was the path to God and heaven. I think of myself as a kind and caring person, but I didn't put a lot of effort into my faith. Sunday church and in times of hardship was status quo. Years passed by, and now I'm 60! For a handful of years, things have been slowly changing and worldly things that didn't bother me before started to nag at me. Our former pastor left due to family health needs, and I found myself neck deep, with a handful of others, searching for a new pastor. I knew that something was missing for me, and I wanted someone who would lead me, teach me, counsel me and encourage me. I got far more than I expected when Pastor Bolton joined our church in April. She opened doors and windows, and introduced me to many amazing people who are on fire for God. I found myself participating in extremely passionate prayer *groups, organizational meetings (equally as passionate) and was asked to be on the Altar Team for the Awake America Crusade. I was raised in a very conservative church environment, so this was very far out of my comfort zone, but something kept pushing me forward. I moved outside my comfort zone, opened my mind and my heart, and I experienced the overwhelming power of the Holy Spirit. I joined the "passionate" people and enjoyed the beautiful, joyful uproar. On the last day of the Crusade, we gathered at the Granville Baptist Church. The passion and joyful uproar were at an all-time high, and there was something "different" happening in the sanctuary! There were things seriously weighing on my heart and mind, and I proceeded to tune out the excitement in the room and went deeply into prayer. As I prayed like I've never prayed before, tears streaming down my face, feeling alone in the roomful of people, I felt what I can only describe as being embraced. I felt like I was being lifted, and this sense of warmth and PURE peace washed over me. I couldn't function and only wanted to bask in the transcendental peace that filled my whole being. This life altering experience, although fleeting, cemented my walk with the Lord and even though my struggles are unresolved, I KNOW that GOD is with me, and HE will show me the way... HIS way!*

"I was able to share this experience with my granddaughter, and on August 10, 2025, we

were both baptized by my pastor, mentor and friend Pamela Bolton in the Mettowee River, recommitting and dedicating ourselves to God!!!"

Dawn Malcahy

"Friday, I brought my dear friend who received a liberating cleansing and healing of emotional wounds.

"While praying for her, the Lord spoke joy, peace, comfort, rest and strength to me in the midst of this aching grieving process of losing my best friend and spouse of 49 years—four years gone this November."

Dawn Waters

"Thank you, Lord. All of us in Rustic Chill we're deeply moved this weekend, simply humble and blessed event."

Heather Kristner

"This meeting did not disappoint. Powerful and holy!"

Carol French

"I want to say thank you to Pamela Bolton for being obedient to God and putting in all the painstaking hours of work and everything that came with planning this Crusade... The prayers that you prayed for so, so many years, they were FINALLY answered. GOD WAS DEFINITELY MOVING throughout the whole Crusade, and as Bishop Lance Johnson said last night, 'WHY NOT????????'

"Come on Upstate New York and all other regions, LETS KEEP THIS GOING !!!!!!!"
Pamela Coon

"Truly amazing and life-changing."
Kathy Ingleston

"It was incredible! God is on the move!"
Margaret Rogers

"Hi, Pastor Bolton.

"I was very moved by the Crusade Thursday evening! So moved that chains were broken off of me, and I experienced deliverance and freedom from the oppression that has been keeping me pinned down from walking in my calling. God gave me confidence and courage after taking me by the hand, lifting me up onto my feet, and embracing me with His love. He said, "I don't make mistakes. You will be everything that I have set a path for you to be. Now get up and step into

what I say and not what the enemy says". It's been a spiritual game changer ever since."
Joseph Bellanger

"Sunday morning I was talking to Pastor Tom Revane about going to the Crusade. But I don't do well with heat and humidity. At that time, we didn't know whether the service was going to be outdoors or indoors, and Pastor Tom was worried about me getting too hot, if I was going to go.

"Well, that morning at church he asked everyone to write down what we wanted to pray about on a Post-it note and put in an envelope. I wrote that I need more time with God in prayer and in his Word.

"At 2 o'clock, we found out that the Crusade service was going to be held inside at the Granville Baptist Church. I told Pastor Tom that I still wanted to go, but to pray about it.

"At 3:30, I had a fire call of a reported structure fire, and it was reported that the building was on fire. Because I'm part of the fire department, I was going to text Pastor Tom and tell him I wasn't going to be able to go, but when the first fire chief arrived on the scene, he found that it was a false alarm. So I was still available to go to the Crusade.

"At 4 o'clock, my phone started sending alerts that there were some severe storms headed our way, so I waited about 5 to 10 minutes to see what was going to happen. But when I was about to text Pastor Tom that I wasn't going to go to the Crusade, I looked outside, and it was sunny with blue skies.

"We finally got up there, and before the service, Bishop Lance announced to everyone that we were going to have some prayer time before the meeting, so I prayed about having more time with God - like I had written and put in the envelope on the Post-it note that morning.

"Then, during the service, Lance did an altar call and said that if anybody needed to come up and just pray at the altar, to do so. I was sitting in the second row, so I decided to pray there, and as I started to pray, my watch started to go off. I took it off, along with my glasses, so as not to get distracted.

"When I bowed my head, there were a lot of people at the altar, but when I was finished praying, everybody had gone back to their seats. I didn't even realize I was that deep in prayer.

"That was the first time, I ever lost track of time while praying. I was praying for something that has been distracting me for quite some time and that I needed to give it to the Lord.

"The next morning at 6 AM, I saw a post by Peter Whitehouse, from the previous day. The post was about some of the things that distract us and out of all the stuff he named, the first thing he said was the thing that I was being distracted by and that I had prayed about during the prayer time with Lance. A little further down in Peter's post, he also stated that we need more time with God in prayer and His Word. That was confirmation that I was supposed to be at that Crusade Sunday, praying for the things that I did. It's just amazing how God can provide a way to tell us we need more of Him. I was called to go to that service on Sunday, and God make sure that I made it there!"

       Greg Fox

Chapter 5

Pastors' Revival Perspectives

Right after the first Crusade meeting, I began to see lots of activity on Facebook regarding this event. People were excited about what God was doing. Pastors were commenting, and there were lots of comments on posts relating to the Crusade. I was thrilled that God was working in pastors' hearts as well as drawing the unsaved and backslidden to Himself.

> *"This is not just a moment;*
> *it is a movement...."*
> *Pastor Rick Setzer*

A PROPHETIC WORD
August 15, 2025

"I was sitting before the Lord tonight outside by my fireplace, and I heard Him say. 'You can't keep a fire going by throwing more kerosene on the flames. It will simply flare up for a moment and quickly burn out.' That is what emotion and hype does for revival. It takes the right kind of dry wood, properly stacked, to sustain it. Prayer, humility, and brokenness is the fuel; and hunger is the flame that sustains the fire of lasting revival."
Prophet Bill Emmons
Prophetic Destiny Ministry and Network
& Life Christian Center, Johnstown, NY

"Knocked me to the ground in His presence and felt his peace and awe."
Pastor Tom Revane
Cornerstone Fellowship, Hoosick Falls, NY

"God got the attention of a man I brought with me. Please pray for Him to continue the work only He can do!

"I went home that night not aware of anything except that it's always a blessing to gather with God's people, to pray and seek His face, to worship, and be edified by the Word of God. I kind of thought, "well, that was nice… now, back to same old same old."

"But yesterday, God "woke me up" to the reality of a remarkably new awareness—not only of God's presence in and with me—but His delight in me as His son and His eagerness to lead me into opportunities to be His witness and work through the agency of my life.

"I find that I am praying more and with greater expectation of seeing God do what only He can do in my life and in the lives of others…praying less out of duty and more out of joyful dependency on Him and the realization that prayer is where the action is.

"The bottom line is, Jesus met me big time at the Friday gathering at Calvary Family Life Center, and I didn't really know it at the time.

"Abba, thank You for Your goodness and mercy! Continue to pour out Your Holy Spirit in upstate New York! Jesus, glorify the Father in Your Body, the Church here! Thank You for opening eyes that we may turn from darkness to light and from the power of Satan to God! Open doors for the Gospel and give utterance to Lance Johnson and all those whom You are raising up to herald the Good News of the Kingdom in this time and place. Seek and save the lost, Jesus, and lead those whom You redeem into deep discipleship and daily fellowship with other believers. Deliver each heart, touched by the power of Jesus Christ in these meetings, we pray, from an evil, unbelieving heart, leading them to fall away from the living God, but surround them with Your people so that they may be exhorted every day, as long as it is called "today," that none of them (or US!) may be hardened by the deceitfulness of sin; in Jesus' name.

"Also, Lance Johnson's teaching about sin as a power that deceives us into believing that we don't want what we most deeply need shined a fresh light on the Gospel for me. There was rich nourishment to be had, and God continues to speak to my heart as I ruminate on the Word proclaimed."

Pastor Dave Martin
Hope United Methodist Church, Troy, NY

"Helped me to know I needed to pray for those I normally wouldn't and that I need Him to teach me how to minister to those I have never encountered but may as time draws near."

"So thankful to God and to all those involved in this Crusade. A time of rejoicing in God our Savior and receiving what He intended each of us to receive. May He continue to grow and strengthen us in our walk with Him, and may the Body of Christ work closer together.

"Thank you so much, Father God!"
Pastor Susan LaFlamme Blocker
Jacob's Well Fellowship, Cambridge, NY

"Healed wounds that happened 28 years ago!!!

"When Lance said there are those that are carrying deep scars, I was quickened by the Holy Spirit to go... my first marriage was 25 years of verbal abuse that ended with my ex-husband threatening me with a gun. He was police officer. That night, I lost my entire family. My husband took our three teenage sons with him. (He had tormented them, too, but he suddenly told them he loved them after years of verbal abuse.) They wanted his love so much. I had tried to protect them from his abuse....but they all wanted a relationship with their dad. They all left before the police came. That was over 28 years ago.

"God healed me over the years, and after several years, my sons came back into my life. I forgave my ex-husband, and over time, we became good friends. Only God can do that!!

"But in my marriage now with my husband, Steve, at times when he would do something similar to my ex-husband, I would find myself reacting... getting angry, bitter, and defensive. Then, recently, after almost losing him twice in the last eight weeks, I was convicted that I can no longer react but that I need to be the loving, patient wife that Jesus wants me to be. So I went to the altar for repentance and freedom, and I felt just absolute freedom, joy, and peace in the Holy Spirit... to be set free from the past and all the years of wounds. Praise God! I am so blessed by what the Holy Spirit did last night. Thank you for all you have done to bring Bishop Lance here. He's coming to Rutland, VT Oct 1 and 2, 2025; and we will never be the same again... Praise Jesus!!!!!"

     Pastor Susie Dumas
Wellspring of Life Christian Center, Rutland, VT

"Refresh!"
Pastor Jacqueline B. Gordon
Granville Baptist Church, Granville, NY

  The crusade proved to be a transformative experience that profoundly deepened my connection with my LORD and God, awakening a passion within me to proclaim the Gospel's message of hope. Similar to the Samaritan woman at the well who couldn't keep for herself what was revealed to her, I felt an overwhelming passion to share the revelation that God revealed to me during the crusade, freely sharing the truth that has transformed my life with anyone my Lord and Savior places in my path.
  Rev. Patricia Medina, Associate Pastor
   Out of the Box Worship Center

"To Pamela Bolton & your incredible team,

  "Please know that eternal things happened not seen by physical eyes in the hearts of hundreds! It was by much prayer and the work of your hands, and YES, America Shall be Saved!

"'Now to Him who is able to do exceedingly abundantly above all that we ask or think, according to the power that works in us, to Him be glory in the church by Christ Jesus to all generations, forever and ever. Amen.' Ephesians 3:20-21"

Crown of Glory Ministries
Evangelists Faye Cohen & Miriam Sumner

"Brothers and Sisters in Christ,

"As I reflect on the incredible time of the body of Christ coming together during the Awake America Crusade, my heart swells with gratitude and excitement for what God is doing among us. This is not just a moment; it is a movement—a divine awakening that stirs our spirits and calls us to action.

"I want to encourage each of you to continue this momentum! The fire that has been ignited within us must not be extinguished. We have witnessed lives transformed, hearts renewed, and souls drawn closer to Christ. This is the work of the Holy Spirit, and it is just the beginning of what God desires to accomplish through us.

"Let us not forget the purpose of this Crusade: to awaken our nation to the truth and love of Jesus Christ. It is a clarion call for each of us to rise up as the body of Christ, united in our mission to bring light into the darkness. We have seen the impact of our collective prayers, our worship, and our outreach efforts, and it is time to build on this foundation.

"Together, we must continue to fill our sanctuaries with heartfelt worship, passionate prayer, and the vibrant energy of community. Bring your friends, your families, your neighbors—invite them into this life-changing experience! Let us continue to baptize in the name of the Father, the Son, and the Holy Spirit, celebrating each new life that comes to know our Savior.

"Now is the time to carry this spirit of awakening beyond the walls of our church. Let us be the hands and feet of Christ in our homes, communities, and workplaces. It is our responsibility to reflect His love and grace in every interaction, to stand firm against the injustices that break the heart of God, and to boldly proclaim the truth of the Gospel in a world that desperately needs hope.

"As we move forward, let us remain steadfast in our commitment to accountability and faith in action. God is calling us to be His instruments of change, to transform our surroundings with the power of His love. Each of you has a vital role to play in this mission, and together, we can make a profound impact on our community and beyond.

"So, I urge you to keep the fire alive! Continue to engage with one another, share your testimonies, and encourage those who may be wavering. We are on this journey together, and the Holy Spirit is guiding us every step of the way.

"Let's not allow the excitement and passion of the Awake America Crusade to fade. Instead, let it propel us into a season of revival, renewal, and outreach. The work has only just begun, and I believe that God has great things in store for us as we press forward in faith.
With all my love and encouragement,
Pastor Rick Setzer
North Bennington Baptist Church, VT
White Creek: Jermain UMC, White Creek, NY
Pownel Center Church, Pownel, Pownel, VT

"What a moment! As we left last night, the singing from inside the church spilled out onto the street, filling the air with praise to God. We stood there, captivated. It was truly a beautiful sound pouring out of the church."
Pastor Liz and David Write
Cornerstone Fellowship, Hoosick Falls, NY

"God, set me free from bad memories (torment).

"During the Crusade, I talked with the Lord, telling Him that I didn't want to leave the same way I came in, and He certainly did not disappoint me. In October of 2021, my husband of almost 50 years changed his address; He is with Jesus now. But God has healed my heart of the traumatic experience that it was for me, and I love to pray!! I did before too, but now it's different, and God did it. He's given me more hunger for Him. All Glory to Him."

"Even bad dreams have stopped."
"There were things that I would dream about... some good, but things from the past started coming into my dreams, and they weren't good... things that I thought had been dealt with, but I had stuffed them deep... and God has healed me.

"God was healing my soul.

"And when Bishop Lance said what he said about deep hurts and trauma, I knew that the Holy Spirit was drawing me, and I was obedient and went up. I immediately started weeping, and I remember Bishop Lance saying something about bad memories as he put his hand in the palm of my hand... and God took it!!! I surrendered to God.

"I Praise and Thank God!!!!"

Pastor Mary Bourne
Wellspring of Life Christian Center, Rutland, VT

"Personal observations regarding our recent New York Crusade for America Program:

"When I was first approached to participate with our churches in the Crusade for America program I had many questions. My wife and I have been involved with Evangelism efforts in three different countries over the years and have experienced a wide range of results. These initiatives range from active participation in a Billy Graham Crusade in England to individual church outreach for newly planted churches in Romania. We were introduced to Bishop Lance Johnson and were intrigued by the effectiveness of his previous crusade efforts. My reaction also included a need to know the man personally, so we invited him to lunch. He was happy to join us, and we got to know Lance personally. I was encouraged to see that this man, who could stand up in front of thousands and proclaim Jesus, was also a humble and practical man of God.

"The preparations for the Crusade in New York were extensive with many church meetings, a lot of prayer and a lot of administration, of which I was involved with only a small portion. Throughout the multi month process, I was impressed with the diligence of the assembled team locally, its leadership and its attention to detail. One of the most positive aspects of the Crusade was seeing a diverse collection of churches come together and agree on the purposes of Christ for our area. A total of 24 churches came together to support this outreach initiative. A strengthening of working relationships between our various churches and the recognition that proclaiming Christ overwhelmed any minor differences we have between denominations and local churches. I personally experienced numerous, encouraging personal affirmations of unity between church leaders during our various meetings.

"During one of the rare quiet periods of our weeklong program, a reporter from a local Newspaper asked me some questions. One of his concerns was whether Christianity was outdated given our current scientific understanding of creation and life itself. Given the subject is one of interest to me, I was pleased to give him an overview of the amazing evidence that confirms the Bible's truth, and the reality that God is real, that he created us, that he created us for his good purposes and that he sent his only Son as our Savior. I do know this, he took a lot of notes, and hopefully that will help him and others in their spiritual journey."

Pastor Bill Steinmetz
Granville Assembly of God, Granville, NY

"The recent revival meetings that were held in our area have continued to fan the flames of revival that are sweeping across our nation.

"Morning 'Gathering of the Lions' training and equipping meetings were held at the Granville Baptist Church. These meetings brought together leaders from 28 churches for intercession, praise, teachings and inspiration. There was such a strong bond of unity and steadfast love that united us and this spilled over into our evening meetings which resulted in many coming to know The Lord and a renewed commitment to serve Him to reach others with His Love.

"One evening meeting in particular provided a unique backdrop for one of our services when over 270 people filled the sanctuary at the Granville Baptist Church where The Holy Spirit fell so strongly that there was no preaching at all as many were overcome by the presence or Our Lord. Signs and wonders followed as the meeting lingered deep into the night and was punctuated by spontaneous praise and worship as we drew near to God and He drew near to us!

"These meetings have continued at various locations throughout our area ever since and they further punctuate that God is on the move in these last days before His return"

Pastor Dan Poucher
Granville Baptist Church, Granville, NY

The night the revival service was held at the Granville Baptist Church was particularly significant to me. Growing up in that church, I had learned who Jesus was and asked Him into my heart as a young child. I had never, however, experienced the presence of the Holy Spirit as palpably as I did that night. I thank Bishop Johnson for recognizing what God was doing, setting aside his preparations, and submitting to God's move. The Holy Spirit brought unity and direction to us that night as a body of believers. As a whole, I believe His children left that service feeling encouraged, edified, and revived!

Joanne Kingsley, Former Pastor

First, I want to thank my precious Lord and Savior for His tenderness and kindness to me. I am thankful for my salvation and how He called me to follow Him from a young age.

During the last night of the Awake America Crusade, there was a call to prayer for leaders and pastors. I had already sensed the moving of the Holy Spirit earlier in the day and had spoken to Pastor Pam about what I felt about what the Lord might do in the service. I had no explicit knowledge, just an inner feeling that it might be quite different from what God had been doing in the previous meetings. As we gathered for prayer, I felt the moving of the Holy Spirit over me. He touched me in a cloud type of feeling, washing over me and regenerating my heart that had been becoming calloused. I still loved God and His people, however not with my usual openness. I had gone through trials, hurts, and many losses as well as disappointments.

It was the next day when I knew He had done a new work of refreshing in me, and I felt lighter, and My heart was healed. I sensed the joy of the Lord again, anew and afresh, and wondered how many others had experienced this same move of the Spirit upon themselves, also. We are all being transformed into the image of Christ. Thank you, Lord, for your love for me.

Pastor Cindylee Bohley
Living Waters Evangelistic Ministries
and Jacob's Well Fellowship, Cambridge, NY

Chapter 6
Worship Team Perspectives

―――◆―――

"For a couple of years, we - the Relevate Worship Team - have been traveling some with Bishop Lance Johnson to various locations that God has handpicked to fan the flames of revival.

"This trip marked the farthest we have traveled, and our hearts were full of expectation. We were excited to join with the body of Christ and labor together in building The Kingdom.

"On the first night, revival services were held inside a historic church that was originally constructed in 1874. It was packed with approx. 300 people and no central AC, yet the presence of God made every moment worth it. The hunger for Him in the room was tangible. I knew that the ground we were standing on had been saturated by generations of prayer.

"Jesus was in the room. And where the Spirit of the Lord is, there is freedom. In that place, beyond race, age, or denomination, there was only one focus—JESUS.

"The following night the Crusade was at the outdoor amphitheater, and in truth, I don't know that I have ever felt so close to God. All creation came together in one accord to give God the glory. Every son and daughter, the wind, and trees, the rhythm of the water and even the way the sun was setting was all for the glory of Jesus.

"Over the course of those two nights, many lives were saved, and the flames of revival were fanned—not only in New York, but within each of our own hearts.

"To God be the glory for all He has done and all He is still doing."
Lanneshia Familuji - Relevate Worship Leader
Relevate Church, Ranger, GA

"I had the opportunity to lead the worship for the last two nights of the four-night crusade. The third night was very special. The worship was full of joy and exuberance. I was delighted to lead worship with Pastor Derik Bartholomew of Cornerstone Outreach Center and Pastor Jason LaPierre of Kingsway Worship Center. Each of us led songs that were so anointed and Spirit led, and then the word that Bishop Lance Johnson brought was deep and convicting. However, my favorite part of the night was after the message and the altar call. We began to worship again and people came to the altar, and many just stayed to soak in the presence after they had received prayer. A baptism team had come with a portable tank, and we worshipped through the baptisms. Each time someone came up from the water, we rejoiced together. There was such a sweet presence the entire time, and people stayed up at the altar worshipping with us until finally we were told that it was time for the town quiet hours and we had to stop.

"The third night was fantastic, but what God did the fourth night went above and beyond. That final night, we had to move to Granville Baptist Church due to the weather. Moving into the church caused us to have to reset the sound system. The reset caused several technical difficulties with the system, especially with my keyboard. After we began the service, I realized that the pedal on the keyboard was not working at all, and the sound had changed from a piano to a synthesizer. I found this extremely distracting, and I was really struggling to continue to sing and play. I actually gave up after the third song, got on my knees and just worshipped; I stopped leading and just let it go. Another musician finished with two more songs, but even his mic kept cutting in and out. However, the presence of God was not hindered in any way by our technical difficulties. In fact, it was so thick that I was overcome. After he played two final songs, we just stopped. Pretty soon, a holy hush began to fall over crowd.

"Something was happening, and we all knew it, and no one wanted to touch it. After the silence, a roar began - a sound of praise began to erupt of people just singing in the Spirit that turned to shouting and praising with everything we had. As I jumped to my feet, I was just singing in tongues at the top of my lungs and tears were running down my face. The thought I had was - thank you, Jesus - for stopping me from trying to manage or control this or try to make something happen in my own strength. I was on my knees in complete surrender when this Holy Spirit moment was able to happen. I had given up - I knew I had nothing to give. I knelt broken before the King.

"Our whole team was undone. Multiple instruments and mics were not working right; we had nothing to offer but our hearts, and God answered with a presence encounter that marked us all. And I'm so grateful. My prayer is that I can listen and sense what He wants to do in a service and how He wants to move, but it's sometimes hard to hear when I'm concentrating on singing and playing. God is really teaching me to let go and trust Him, and know that He always comes through."

Heather Bartos - Worship Pastor
Connect Church Assembly of God, Hartwick, NY

"In July, I had the opportunity to travel to NY to be a part of the team for the Awake America Crusade. I went with great expectations for what God was going to do, and because He is so faithful, He exceeded any expectation that I could ever set!

"The first night of the crusade was absolute fire! You could feel the expectation in the air, the people were hungry and you could literally feel it. We watched as these hungry warriors poured out their hearts to the Lord! It has forever marked and changed me!

"By Saturday morning, all I could do was lay on my face before the Lord! His presence was so thick and tangible! He called me to a deeper place in Him, a deeper trust! When you go to serve at an event like this, you expect to pour out, but in Whitehall, NY, not only did I have the honor to pour out the heart of Jesus, but so much more was poured into me! I know that God has started something new in Upstate NY. What He has started will transform this region! I cannot wait to see Him do what only He can do!"
 Jennifer Davis - Relevate Worship Team, Relevate Church, Ranger, GA

Chapter 7

Follow-Up News Articles

Awake America Crusade brings faith, music, and renewal to Whitehall

A worshiper raises her hands and sways along with worship music during the Awake America Crusade held July 17-20 in Whitehall. The Crusade is intended to help people who may have strayed from the path of God find their way back, said Crusade organizer Pamela Bolton, pastor of Whitehall's Out of the Box Worship Center.

WHITEHALL – Four days of prayer, preaching and songs of praise filled air last week as the Awake America Crusade came to Whitehall, reviving what had been a common occurrence in the late 1800s but had faded away for much of the 20th century.

More than 300 worshipers packed into the sweltering First Baptist Church in Whitehall on the first day of the four-day Awake America Crusade on July 17. The first day of the event was moved indoors because of the threat of thunderstorms...

    The crusade was a modern version of the Billy Graham crusades of the 1940s through the early 2000s and the revival meetings of a century before – including a "massive revival" that filled the Brick Church on County Route 18 to overflowing in the late 1800s, said Pamela Bolton, pastor of the Out of the Box Worship Center in Whitehall and the primary organizer of the current crusade.

Lance Johnson, a bishop from Georgia who travels the country preaching at revival meetings, preaches during the Awake America Crusade in Whitehall on July 18.

Musicians and singers from Lance Johnson Ministries respond to the crowd of roughly 300 that gathered in the Skenesborough Drive Park Amphitheater perform worship songs during the Awake America Crusade on July 18.

The crusade, like the earlier religious happenings, is intended to help people who may have strayed from the path of God, Bolton said. "We want people to have their hearts turned back to God," she said.

"We want people to know how much he loves them,' said Ed Bartos of Cooperstown, who was working as a volunteer helping people find parking for the event. "It's all about Jesus," he said.

"I believe we're going to see revival in America," said Lance Johnson, a bishop from Georgia who served as one of the worship leaders of the event. "He's not done with this great nation."

More than 300 worshipers packed into the sweltering First Baptist Church on July 17, the first day of the event, after organizers moved the services from the Skenesborough Drive Park amphitheater because of looming thunderstorms.

The hot, crowded conditions did little to reduce the enthusiasm of those who attended, as they swayed to the worship music and listened intently to the messages of faith and hope.

The services returned to the amphitheater for the final days of the event, bringing with them the fervor that attendees had shown the first day.

The amphitheater was chosen to host the crusade in the hopes that the event would draw people just walking or driving by to come in and hear the message, Bolton said. The event is not just about spreading the word that God loves them, but also about helping anyone in need deal with the troubles plaguing their lives, she said.

Destiny Negron of Glens Falls said he was one of those helped by God, explaining why he had traveled to Whitehall for the crusade. Just a few years ago, Negron said he had used a utility knife to slice his forearm in his car in the parking lot of his workplace because of all the troubles in his life. But, Negron said, when he looked up from making the cuts, he saw what appeared to be the words "I am" formed by the foliage of a surrounding hedge.

"He spoke to me, and I have been following him" since that day, Negron said, showing a photo in which the letters can be seen in the brush. He has made it his mission to help people who – like him – had despaired but could find a path forward through Jesus, he said.

"I just love helping people," he said, adding "I like to see transformed faces" when his message resonates with people."

Negron said he is now studying to become a pastor himself.
By EJ Conzola II, NYVT Media – *Sentinel Times*
Published July 23, 2025 at 3:00 PM; Photo Credits, too. Used with permission.

Outpouring Whitehall, NY: Awake America Crusade Ignites Regional Awakening

Over four unforgettable days in Whitehall and Granville, New York, a powerful spiritual revival broke out during the Awake America Crusade. It ignited a movement that many had prayed for over decades. This wasn't just another church event; it was a divine visitation. A true outpouring of God's presence that is still rippling through Upstate New York and beyond.

"I'm sitting on a plane this morning still trying to wrap my mind around everything God did," said Bishop Lance Johnson, evangelist and founder of Lance Johnson Ministries. "Over 200 saved, and the last night was history-making as God poured out His Spirit and marked us all with His marvelous glory. I am humbled and undone."

Held in the towns of Whitehall and Granville, the Awake America Crusade brought together over 60 pastors and over 300 attendees. It marked the culmination of more than two decades of prayer and preparation by regional leaders.

From Prayer to Regional Awakening

Pastor Pamela Bolton of South Granville Congregational Church and Out of the Box Worship Center, recalls how her passion to see revival in our day began approximately 25 years ago when she watched a documentary called *Transformations* on revival and began praying for a move of God. Her heart was stirred. Then in 2019, she called for regional prayer along the New York–Vermont border. She gathered pastors and believers across denominational lines, who were crying out for revival. "We met in a historic old brick church erected in 1826 in Whitehall with no electricity and no running water," she said. "People brought scripture, testimonies, and prayers—there was so much unity, you could feel God's presence the moment you walked in the door."

JULY 20, 2025 - GRANVILLE BAPTIST CHURCH

When Bishop Lance came to the area to do a series of meetings in the summer of 2024, he felt led by the Lord to launch a regional crusade. He asked Pastor Jason LaPierre, Pastor Timothy Bohley, and Pastor Pamela Bolton to help organize it. What followed was a powerful partnership that laid the foundation for what became the Awake America Crusade.

Revival Continues at Kingsway Worship Center

Pastor Jason Lapierre, of Kingsway Worship Center, who first invited Bishop Lance to the region, witnessed revival continue after the Crusade ended. At Kingsway Worship Center in Hudson Falls, NY, the Sunday following the Crusade, the Spirit of God fell powerfully.

"We baptized all kinds of people," he said. "Sunday morning, the glory of God hit, and we just kept going. People were baptized in the Holy Spirit—and we never planned any of it." He added, "We were supposed to be in New York City on Monday, but when the glory hit, we knew we had to stay. Bishop Lance confirmed it; he told us to keep going, so we did."

Jason recalled that the final night hosted by Pastor Dan Poucher at the Granville Baptist Church was especially powerful. "The glory of God came in the room. That was the most incredible service for me. For a moment, it felt like we were drawn into the Holy of Holies. I've never experienced anything like it."

A Movement of Unity and Fire

Pastor Rick Setzer encouraged the body of Christ in a public letter: "Let us not forget the purpose of this Crusade—to awaken our nation to the truth and love of Jesus Christ. This is not just a moment; it is a movement."

Pastor Jason Proctor of Ballston Spa United Methodist Church, who lives in Corinth, NY, echoed that sentiment. He said, "I've lived in rural upstate New York for 17 years. I've never seen anything like this. This is not a professional, organized religious event. This is a family on fire crying out for the healing love of God to shine on a starving generation."

JULY 19, 2025 - PASTOR JASON LaPIERRE
AT SKENESBOROUGH AMPHITHEATER

LOCAL WORSHIP TEAM
REV. HEATHER BARTOS, PASTOR JASON LaPIERRE,
AND PASTOR DERIK BARTHOLOMEW AND FRIENDS

A Moment That Marked the Region

The final night at Granville Baptist Church left many undone. Bishop Lance stepped aside from his prepared message as a deep hush fell over the sanctuary. The music stopped. Silence filled the room. Many wept, knelt, or simply stood in awe. It was a moment of sacred encounter.

"It was our moment of visitation," Pastor Pamela said. "I've never seen anything like it in all my life. The presence of God filled that place and no one wanted to leave."

JULY 20, 2025 - GRANVILLE BAPTIST CHURCH

JULY 20, 2025 - GRANVILLE BAPTIST CHURCH
THE GLORY OF GOD FILLED THE ROOM

What's Next?
Vermont Leadership Gathering and 2026 Crusade

The next Crusade meeting will be held Friday, August 1st, 6:30 pm, Calvary Assembly of God, 100 Sherman Ave, Glens Falls, NY. Revival is continuing to spread. Plans are underway for a major Vermont New Hampshire Revival Network leadership meeting in Waterbury Center, Vermont, on August 22–23, at Hunger Mountain Christian Assembly. There, pastors and ministry leaders will gather to begin planning the 2026 Vermont Crusade.

"There were over 100 volunteers," Pastor Pamela added. Over 300 people came each night. Over the course of 4 nights, there were likely over 1,000 different people in attendance. Over 200 souls made commitments to the Lord, either making a first-time commitment or a recommitment, and countless more were touched in ways only heaven can measure."

More importantly, unity remains the hallmark of this move. Worship leaders yielded when the Spirit led otherwise. Churches that had never connected before were now praying, worshiping, and believing together.

It wasn't about platforms or performance. It was about Jesus.

**RELEVATE CHURCH WORSHIP TEAM
JULY 17, 2025 - FIRST BAPTIST CHURCH**

INSIDE FIRST BAPTIST CHURCH, WHITEHALL

A Call to Steward the Move of God

As the Crusade came to a close, Bishop Lance gave a final exhortation: **"Stay low. Stay hungry. Stay humble. Stay broken."**

The fire of revival is burning, and now is the time to tend it. As Pastor Pam put it, "We're nurturing this move of God, and we must protect the move so it stays as God intended."

The revival and awakening have begun. May it continue in every church, every home, and every heart.

FIRST BAPTIST CHURCH - FIRST NIGHT OF CRUSADE

INSIDE FIRST BAPTIST CHURCH, WHITEHALL
JULY 17, 2025, FIRST BAPTIST CHURCH, WHITEHALL

JULY 17, 2025, FIRST BAPTIST CHURCH, WHITEHALL ALTAR CALL

**INSIDE FIRST BAPTIST CHURCH, WHITEHALL
JULY 17, 2025, FIRST BAPTIST CHURCH, WHITEHALL**

**JULY 19, 2025, BAPTISM
SKENESBOROUGH AMPHITHEATER, WHITEHALL**

SKENESBOROUGH AMPHITHEATER, WHITEHALL, NY

The author is the pastor of the Church of the Crucified One in Moretown, Vermont, and the publisher of *MyFaithNews*. Used with permission.

CHAPTER 8

PHOTO ALBUM

A PICTURE IS WORTH A THOUSAND WORDS

JULY 20, 2025 – GRANVILLE BAPTIST CHURCH

JULY 17, 2025 – FIRST BAPTIST CHURCH

JULY 17, 2025 FIRST BAPTIST CHURCH, WHITEHALL

JULY 17, 2025 FIRST BAPTIST CHURCH, WHITEHALL

SKENESBOROUGH AMPHITHEATER

JULY 19, 2025 – HEATHER BARTOS

JULY 19, 2025 – JASON LaPIERRE, HEATHER BARTOS, DERIK BARTHOLOMEW AND FRIENDS

SKENEBOROUGH AMPHITHEATER ALTAR CALL

SKENESBOROUGH AMPHITHEATER BAPTISM

SKENESBOROUGH AMPHITHEATER

SKENESBOROUGH AMPHITHEATER

JULY 20, 2025 – GRANVILLE BAPTIST CHURCH

JULY 20, 2025 – GRANVILLE BAPTIST CHURCH

AUGUST 1, 2025 - CALVARY'S FAMILY LIFE CENTER

**CALVARY'S FAMILY LIFE CENTER
PASTOR BILL HARRINGTON**

**CALVARY'S FAMILY LIFE CENTER
BISHOP LANCE JOHNSON**

CALVARY'S FAMILY LIFE CENTER

A LITTLE HISTORY
GOD IS DOING IT AGAIN!

BURLEIGH'S GIFT TO RELIGION

The ex-Congressman Donates a Y. M. C. A. Building at Whitehall, N. Y.

WHITEHALL, N. Y., March 24—The religious revival conducted by W. E. Geil, of Doylestown, Pa., at which 450 persons professed conversion, was closed to-night. All the stores and saloons in Whitehall were closed during the evening last week.

Mr. Geil announced to-night that ex-Congressman H. G. Burleigh had offered to donate the building occupied by the Young Men's Christian Association, together with the land, if $2,000 was raised to enlarge and equip it. A popular subscription was started, and in twenty minutes the $2,000 was raised. In less than an hour $625 more had been added to supply furniture and books. Including Mr. Burleigh's gift, the amount raised in four hours was over $7,000.

The Elizabethtown Post, 28 March 1895 — Page 4

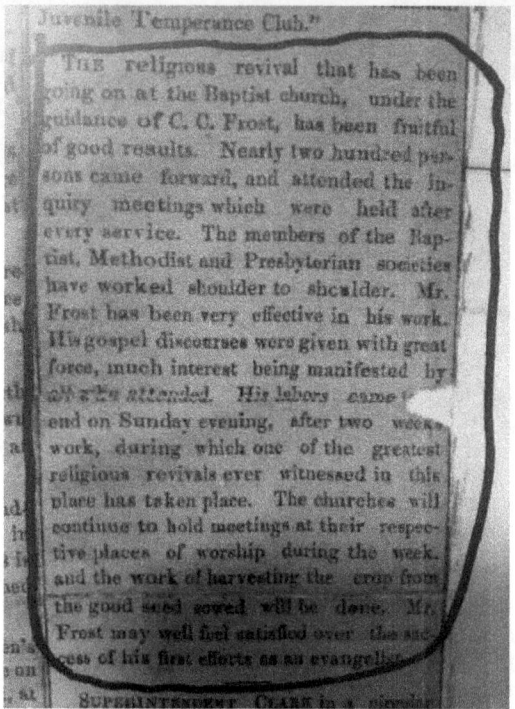

Courtesy of the Historical Society of Whitehall
1895 - Found in an old scrapbook

EVANGELIST GEIL'S MEETINGS.

Evangelist Wm. E. Geil, of Doylestown, Pa., is holding meetings of great interest at Northville. The community for miles around is deeply stirred, stores and saloons being closed each evening and everyone attending the services.

Mr. Geil is a local preacher of the Methodist church, of boyish appearance. He has been most successful in this part of the state. At Schenectady there were 400 converts, at Broadalbin 350, at Warrensburgh 250, at Mayfield 250, at Granville 300. From Northville Mr. Geil will go to Fort Edward for two weeks.

The Johnstown Daily Republican, 10 September 1894

CHAPTER 9
NOW WHAT?

SEEK THE LORD WITH ALL YOUR HEART; SPEND TIME WITH HIM!

YOU MATTER TO GOD!

More than anything else, Jesus wants to spend time with you. He wants you to know how much He loves and values you, and He wants to reveal Himself to you in greater measure. He wants to hear from you, and He wants you to learn to hear His voice more clearly.

In the Bible, Jesus said that His sheep know His voice, and scripture also says that those who are led by the Spirit of God are the sons (and daughters) of God. (John 10:27 and Romans 8:14) God desires that we learn to recognize His voice and that we be led by the Holy Spirit.

HE FORMED YOU WITH A PLAN AND SPECIAL PURPOSE FOR YOUR LIFE!

The Word of the Lord to the prophet, Jeremiah: *"**Before I formed you in the womb, I knew you; Before you were born, I sanctified you; I ordained you a prophet to the nations."*** Jeremiah 1:5 (NKJV)

"For I know the thoughts that I think toward you, says the Lord, thoughts of peace and not of evil, to give you a future and a hope." Jeremiah 29:11 (NKJV)

God had a plan for Jeremiah's life before He even formed him in the womb. He had a plan for the disciples' lives, and He has a plan for your life as well.

WALK IN YOUR CALLING & FULFILL YOUR CALL

"What is my purpose or my call?"

It is partially your position in your family, but it goes far beyond that. Each one of us was born with a call on our lives, to make a difference for eternity. Many people just don't realize how important their calls are.

If you don't already know what yours is, you need to seek God about this. He wants to fill you with His Spirit, reveal your call to you, and empower you to walk in it. He created you for relationship with Him and to walk in your calling!

If our forefathers hadn't walked in their callings, God would have given their God-given purposes to others. He will find a way for His will to be accomplished on Earth; however, He may need to do it differently than His first plan, because we have free will. The choice is ours, whether or not to walk in our call. He won't force us.

Each of our lives is intertwined with many other people. We all have a circle of influence. If we look at every day as an opportunity to partner with God, then we will realize that He wants to use us to make a difference for His Kingdom.

Remember that God often used people who didn't measure up to the standards of the "religious" people of the time in which they were living in. He specializes in using those who feel unqualified or who don't think they measure up to the world's standards.

*For you see your calling, brethren, that **not many wise according to the flesh, not many mighty, not many noble, are called**. But God has chosen the foolish things of the world to put to shame the wise, and God has chosen the weak things of the world to put to shame the things which are mighty; and the base things of the world and the things which are despised God has chosen, and the things which are not, to bring to nothing the things that are, that no flesh should glory in His presence. But of Him you are in Christ Jesus, who became for us wisdom from God—and righteousness and sanctification and redemption—that, as it is written, "He who glories, let him glory in the LORD."* 1 Corinthians 1:26-31 (NKJV)

I love this quote by Smith Wigglesworth because it sums up how God operates:

**"God does not call those who are equipped;
He equips those whom He has called."**

**Continue to seek God's face,
pray for full-blown revival and awakening,
believe Him for greater things,
and walk in your calling!**

.

THANK YOU!

**MOST IMPORTANTLY:
THANK YOU, JESUS, FOR MOVING IN POWER THROUGHOUT THE ENTIRE CRUSADE AND IN AN EXTRAORDINARY WAY ON THE LAST EVENING!**

After this, I want to begin by saying that there were literally over 100 people who volunteered and helped make the Awake America Crusade possible. Every single one of you mattered and made a difference! There were those who faithfully attended the prayer events and prayed at home as well as weekly in their individual churches, and every sincere prayer mattered to God! Look at the results!

With that being said, I want to begin by expressing my deepest appreciation to several groups of people and individuals who served and/or oversaw different areas of ministry.

First, I want to thank Pastors Jason and Tammie LaPierre for heading up the Altar Ministry Team; Second, Pastor Bill Harrington and his wife, Lisa, for heading up the Ushers, Greeters, and Parking Attendants Teams; Third, Pastor Tim Bohley and Jef Bourn for heading up the Clean-up Crew; and Fourth, Heather Bartos for leading the local Praise and Worship Team as well as the Children's Ministry Team. Lots of time and energy went into planning and preparation so that the Crusade meetings would run smoothly, and they did. You all were amazing!

Thank you, Father Leo Benjamin, for all of the hours that you spent writing articles and doing interviews to help promote the Crusade. All of your hard work was invaluable!

I also want to thank Bruce Turco and Team for building an extension on both sides of the platform at Skenesborough

Amphitheater (in extreme heat). Your time and all of your efforts were greatly appreciated!

Tommy and Mary Beth Finn, thank you for lovingly preparing and delivering the food for the leadership meetings. You blessed many people with your amazing cooking!

A big THANK YOU to both First Baptist Church and Granville Baptist Church for allowing us to hold services at your locations. Your hospitality was crucial to the success of the Crusade; and thank you, too, Calvary Life Center for hosting the first follow-up Crusade meeting. I also want to recognize the two churches that allowed us to hold pre-crusade meetings, First Baptist Church and Faith Chapel, both in Whitehall. Thank you!

Last but not least, I also want to thank Bishop Lance Johnson and his ministry team who came and served us tirelessly and selflessly. You all were a wonderful blessing to the people of upstate New York and Vermont, and I believe that your passion for and dedication to the Lord will make a huge difference for the Kingdom of God, in our region, for years to come.

In Closing

I pray that this book has challenged you to seek the Lord with everything that's in you and about the seriousness of your commitment level to God. Are you completely sold out for Jesus? Remember that God wants to draw you closer to Himself, reveal Himself in greater measure to you right now, and to use YOU for Kingdom purposes ... FOR A SUCH A TIME AS THIS.

May God bless you, prepare you, strengthen you, lead you, guide you, give you wisdom, and use you to help bring in the final harvest of souls in these last days in which we're living.

SALVATION PRAYER

If you don't already know Jesus as your Lord and Savior and you want to, please pray the following prayer from your heart to enter into a relationship with Him:

Dear Jesus,
    I admit that I'm a sinner, and I need You. Thank you for dying on the cross in my place and taking my punishment. Please forgive me for my sins, and come into my heart and be my Savior and my Lord. Please help me to live for You from this day forward. Thank you for making me part of Your family. In Jesus' Name, Amen.

If you prayed this prayer sincerely from your heart, you are now a child of God. You have just taken your first step in your journey with Him. Welcome to His family.

www.ingramcontent.com/pod-product-compliance
Lightning Source LLC
Chambersburg PA
CBHW070503100426
42743CB00010B/1742